Chaos & the Kingdom

Chaos & the Kingdom

Nathanael Vissia

&

Michael Bush

A *Reign of God* book

Book design by Nathanael Vissia

Image book cover art:
Colorful ink in water
© Leigh Prather | Dreamstime.com

ISBN   978-0-9963336-0-3
eISBN 978-0-9963336-1-0

rfour publishing
www.rfourpublishing.com

This book is dedicated to Henriet Vissia & Marti Bradford Goodall

Special thanks to
Christine Durst, Amy Stillman Kulig, Martha Parrish Bush,
& The United Church of Christ at Valley Forge

Contents

Introduction

Jesus came to Galilee, proclaiming the good news of God, and saying, "The time is fulfilled, and the kingdom of God has come near; repent, and believe in the good news."

Mark 1:14-15

◻ ◻ ◻ ◻ ◻ ◻

Have you noticed how certain perceptions of God, Jesus and Christianity affect America's tone and direction in international, domestic, economic and political affairs?

We have. And we are concerned by this marriage of politics and Christianity that distorts the image and identity of God, Jesus, the Bible, and the Church.

We have also noticed how using scripture and religious beliefs to support or argue a political position propagates the fallacy that God, Jesus, and the Church validate one type of an "earthly kingdom" over another.

In other words, the Good News that Jesus proclaimed has been leveraged by interest groups, governments, corporations and, yes, even churches, to win culture wars, legislate morality, and rationalize votes for political parties.

1

But this is not the Good News. The Good News is not about political power. It is not about forcing people to live a certain way. Furthermore, the Good News is not that Jesus and God love us.

Wait...WHAT did you just say? Did you just say that God doesn't love me? That JESUS doesn't love me?

Hello, dear reader and welcome to the discussion. Although we understand your concern, that isn't quite what we said. Yes, of course God and Jesus love you, but God's love for us is *not* the Good News that Jesus proclaimed.

That's blasphemy! Aren't you worried that you will go to hell for saying such things?

Well, since you've brought it up: The idea that Jesus is our personal Lord and Savior, who, if we believe in him, will be the reason we enter heaven (instead of hell) is *still* not the Good News that Jesus proclaimed.

What are you talking about!? Why should I read one more word of your book that is so obviously NOT based on the Bible?

Oh, but it is based on the Bible! And if you leave now, you won't hear the actual Biblically-based Good News that Jesus preached.

Then what IS the Biblically-based Good News?

In the Gospel[1] according to Mark, we are told that Jesus began his ministry "proclaiming the good news of God, and saying, 'The time is fulfilled, and the kingdom of God has come near; repent, and believe in the good news. ' "[2]

The Good News, the focus of Jesus' ministry, and why Jesus calls us to follow him are all centered on this: *"The kingdom of God has come near!"*

But you just said that hanging out with God after we die isn't the Good News!?

We did just say that.

So are you saying that "heaven" and "the kingdom of God" are different?

Yes, that *is* what we are saying. What most people mean by "heaven" is a human imagining of what happens to us after we die. The kingdom of God, however, is *wherever we let God be king.*

---

[1] The word "Gospel" means, "Good news"
[2] Mark 1:14-15

When Jesus says it is near, he's saying the kingdom of God can be experienced and shared right here, right now, while we are *alive*. And, when we experience it, like Jesus did, like his disciples did, then we are able to live into and share God's love and power just like they did.

How is that possible? God is in *heaven* and we are *here*. We experience heaven when we DIE, not while we're alive.

It sounds like you are still confusing "heaven" with "kingdom." We are not saying that there is no heaven; we are saying that "the kingdom of God" and "heaven" are different concepts to keep separate. A possible reason for why we conflate the two ideas is because the phrase, "kingdom of God," can evoke fanciful images of a far-away never-never land – which can seem a lot like what heaven could be.

But the word *baseilea* – the Greek word in the Gospels which is translated to English as "kingdom" – does not primarily refer to a geographic area. Instead, *baseilea* refers to the authority and influence given to a particular person. In other words, the kingdom of God does not refer to a place, but to God's reign – meaning that whenever and wherever we receive God's guidance/power/spirit, *that* is where the kingdom of God is.[3]

---

[3] Note that we will use the phrase "The reign of God" interchangeably with "The kingdom of God" throughout the book.

Whoa – just a minute, now! This is a new idea that leaves me feeling uncomfortable. How do I know if I'm in God's kingdom or not? Is it like getting into heaven? If so, then I'm in! I've been confirmed and gone on mission trips. I have professed Jesus as my Lord and Savior. I once read the entire Bible in one year. I attend worship services regularly and practice random acts of kindness. Isn't that enough? Doesn't that mean I'm in God's kingdom?

We learn how to let God reign in our lives by following Jesus.

Then I'm good! Like I said – I've professed Jesus as my Lord and Savior.

But there's abundantly more to following Jesus than professing him as your Lord and Savior.

Abundantly more!? What more could there be to being saved?

A sentence or a paragraph would not adequately address your question. That is why we are inviting you to participate in a conversation about it.

A conversation?

Yes, a conversation that will clarify how we are to follow Jesus, why we would choose to do so, as well as what Jesus saves us from and for.

And how will we do that?

By focusing on one well-known Bible story per chapter and discussing the important role that chaos plays in that story.

Chaos? There aren't any Bible stories about chaos – well-known or otherwise!

We think you'll be surprised by how central the role of chaos is in these six Bible stories. We also think you'll appreciate how the recognition of chaos' role in these stories can strongly reshape our understandings of those stories, as well as our perspective of God, the kingdom of God, Jesus, the disciples, and ourselves. We'll discuss related topics, too, like God's intention for creation, what salvation is, and the identity of Jesus. We'll even talk a little bit about unclean spirits.

That *does* sound interesting. Since this is going to be a conversation, can I keep asking you questions?

Of course! But our greatest hope is that the book will help facilitate discussions between you and your fellow group members.

Group members? What group members?

This book can be read alone, but we affirm Jesus' teaching that "where two or three are gathered in my name, I am there among them"[4] and, therefore, believe that a community effort is the best way to think and learn about the truth of God. We're also mindful of Paul's description of the Body of Christ, which we will summarize as: *The more of us who gather together, the more complete the Body is.*[5]

With these thoughts in mind, we've created a chapter structure that will support and facilitate small-group discussion. Each chapter consists of these components:

Context – This section offers some historical, cultural and Biblical insights for the chapter's scripture story.

Scripture Passage – We recommend, after the *Opening Question* (to be explained soon), that one person in class reads the scripture as printed in each chapter. The scripture that is included is from the New Revised Standard Version.

Concepts – This section will describe a few ideas that appear either in the scripture reading or in the following *Ruminations* section. Language (i.e., the naming of things) defines how we see, think, and feel. If we all have different

---

[4] Matthew 18:20
[5] 1 Corinthians 18:8-12

understandings of a concept – like "sin," for instance – then conversation becomes quite difficult, if not impossible. By sharing our understanding of a concept, we hope to reduce some of this difficulty.

Ruminations – Even with the story in front of us, nestled between historic context and defined concepts, the narrative of the story and its relevance to us is not always crystal-clear. By no means will all of the layers and threads that run through each scripture story be covered in this section. But we will address how the main theme of the book (chaos) is present in the chapter's scripture passage, and also show how it echoes, reinforces, and adds to discussions and stories from the previous chapters. We'll also throw in an opinion or two.

Suggested Outline for Class Discussion – This section appears at the end of each chapter and offers a suggested order for the group discussion after each chapter. It includes:

Opening Question – This question offers an opportunity for the participants to share personal stories that will also relate to at least one of the topics from that chapter.

Discussion Questions – Listed in this section will be a number of questions to help prompt group discussion. These questions are designed to elicit responses from you and your fellow group members regarding the ideas that were shared in the chapter. The questions might also affirm or challenge personally-held beliefs and perspectives about God, Jesus, the Holy Spirit, the Church, the Bible, and characters in the Bible. Our hope is that the conversations will consist more of clarifying remarks (i.e., sharing how you understood the chapter) and personal experiences (e.g., how the chapter challenged you; what you appreciated; personal stories that seem relevant to the chapter) rather than attempts to convert others to a particular perspective (i.e., arguing).

Closing Prayer – Closing prayer is a chance for classmates to lift in prayer the topics and questions that were raised during the class discussion as well as any other joys and concerns.

The structure of each chapter seems helpful – do you have any scheduling suggestions?

We do. Overall, we suggest you set aside seven weeks for the discussions, allowing for one session per chapter. The first week would be to discuss this *Introduction* chapter and plan how to proceed.

When a small group in our local church gathered to discuss the book, they met for an hour. Everyone involved thought that an hour and a half would've been better, but one hour *was* sufficient.

There were groups that used the book before you published it?

Yes, there were. And we are very thankful to everyone who helped. The book is much improved because of the time, effort, and feedback provided by the folks at The United Church of Christ at Valley Forge in Wayne, PA.

Anything else you wish to share about the group's experience?

We strongly suggest that you assign a facilitator, either for the whole study (recommended) or by chapter (more difficult in general, we think, but such an approach does allow for a greater chance of varied perspectives). The role of the facilitator might involve some or all of the following:

- Schedule and/or remind the group of the dates when the group is meeting.

- Set up the room ahead of time.

- Begin the discussions with an opening prayer at the agreed upon starting time.

- Ask the opening question and have an answer ready as a way to encourage sharing within the group.

- Choose which questions (located at the end of the chapter) to ask and then ask them.

- When discussing a question, encourage the group to refer back to the scripture story and text of the chapter. Also, if the group seems to be drifting too far off-topic, remind them of the original question.

- Because a facilitator will know the group better than we do, the facilitator is encouraged to frame or phrase the questions differently than they may be written. The facilitator might also consider offering his/her own follow-up questions as well.

- Facilitate the closing of the discussions with prayer at the agreed-upon ending time.

I'm wary of people I don't know, so tell me – who are you to write such things? What gives you the right, the *authority*, to talk about such topics?

In the Gospel according to Luke, when Gabriel, a messenger of God, reassures Zechariah that he and his wife, Elizabeth, will indeed have a child despite their advanced age, Zechariah inquiries doubtfully, "How can I be sure of this?" Gabriel responds with, "I stand in the presence of the Lord."[6] That seems

---

[6] Luke 1:18-19

like a good answer for us, too: We seek to stand in the presence of the Lord.

Our on-going, ten-plus-years, God-centered friendship (which has been filled with praying, arguing, and working together to share the Good News) has led to the expressed ideas and understandings shared in the following chapters.

Opposite from each other in just about every way, we're more likely to argue than agree, and without God at the center of our friendship, we would not get along. There are also times when one of us despairs or gets lost. But because there are two of us, we hold each other accountable.

As for our professional background:

Michael has served as an ordained pastor for several United Church of Christ congregations for over 20 years. You can listen to his current sermons online at www.uccvf.org/mp3_ sermons. html.

Nathanael has worked in three churches in various Director of Christian Education roles. His website, rfour.org, offers more than 200 free, fully-developed, ready-for-the-classroom Sunday school lessons, over 100 children's time messages for the lectionary cycle, and free adult Bible study guides.

So, you're not the usual Christian book authors who are theologians, professors, or mega-church pastors?

It is true that we do not fit the expected mold which, according to the Bible stories, is what happens when you choose to seek God and live God's way. And so, we invite you to join us in learning, discussing, and experiencing even more of the wonderful, exciting, and unconventional ways of life that God is calling us to live.

Suggested Outline for
CLASS DISCUSSION

1. **Opening Prayer**

2. **Introductions**: Go around the circle and have each person share with the group their name and their favorite TV show or movie that they watched as a child (or feel free to use another/different question)

3. **Briefly share** how each class will proceed, the schedule for the entire study, and create a contact sheet with phone numbers and email addresses.

4. **Discuss** the Introduction chapter with the following questions (or questions of your own):

   a) Was there anything in the *Introduction* chapter that you appreciated, disagreed with, struggled to accept or didn't understand?

   b) After reading the *Introduction*, what do you hope to experience by reading the book and attending the class?

   c) Early in the *Introduction*, a distinction was made between "kingdom of God" and "Heaven." Is this a distinction that you have noted before? Do you see any significance in noting the distinction?

d) Part of the conversation in the book will be about how "There's abundantly more to following Jesus than professing him as your Lord and Savior." What do you understand, personally, to be some of those "more" things?

e) The main theme/topic of the book is about the relationship between God, humans, and chaos. Have you ever thought about chaos in the context of what Christianity might have to say about it? Why or why not?

5. **Discuss details for next class** (e.g., when it will happen and what chapter to read in preparation)

6. **Closing Prayer** (3 to 7 minutes) – Facilitator opens the prayer and then ceases his/her out loud praying to allow members of the group to pray out loud or silently for whatever comes to mind. Facilitator then closes the prayer.

1. Genesis

Babylonians, symbolic water & the Word

■ ❑ ❑ ❐ ❑ ❑

CONTEXT

Traditionally, the authorship of the first five books of the Bible, also known as the "Torah" or "The Law," is attributed to Moses, who is considered to have lived somewhere around 1400 B.C.E. However, the written date of the Torah is now widely agreed upon by Biblical scholars to be somewhere in the mid-500s B.C.E.[7]

This was a dark time for the Israelites. First, their Northern Kingdom of Israel was overrun by Assyria and then, later, their Southern Kingdom of Judah was conquered by the Babylonian Empire. This is when the Temple (built by King Solomon) was destroyed and the treasures of Jerusalem were hauled away to Babylon. The "promised land" was in ruins and many of the Israelites were in exile. God's power was, in the face of

---

[7] Davies, G.I. See resource #9 in Reference List
Brueggemann, W. See resource #6 in Reference List
Enns, P. See resource #10 in Reference List

overwhelming Babylonian force, looking small (at best) and non-existent (at worst) to the Israelites.

It is during this tumultuous time, then, that Genesis is widely-considered to have taken written form. And, because no author works in a vacuum, it is helpful to note the cultural context and current events that inevitably shaped the writing of Genesis.

Take, for instance, the influence of the creation story of the Babylonian religion, known as the *Enuma Elish*. In the *Enuma Elish*, there is a "first" creation that emerges from a formless state and is inhabited solely by two gods, *Apsu* (which means "fresh water") and *Tiamat* (which means "salt water").[8] Eventually, new gods appear and they do battle with these first gods. The champion of the new gods, *Marduk*, leads the attack on *Tiamat*. Here is an excerpt from that scene:

Marduk raises up his rain-flood weapon and challenges Tiamat to single combat. Tiamat loses her temper, accepts the challenge, and advances, all the while shouting spells. Marduk encircles Tiamat with his net, blows her up with his winds, and shoots "an arrow which pierced her belly, / Split her down the middle and slit her heart." Marduk then proceeds to create the universe from Tiamat's body:

---

[8] Some believe *Tiamat* may be the origin of the Hebrew word *tehom* for "the deep" which appears in Genesis 1:2 (Jacobsen, T -- see resource #17 in Reference List.)

He sliced her in half like a fish for drying:
Half of her he put up to roof the sky,

Drew a bolt across and made a guard to hold it.
Her waters he arranged so they could not escape. [9]

This is the creation story that the most powerful empire in the world told itself and others – that all of creation, including humankind, was a product borne of war between the gods. A natural interpretation of such a story, then, was that the human condition, as a product of war, was to continue the fight and overcome all opponents. Certainly, the cultural, economic, and military might of the Babylonians in the 500s B.C. provided convincing proof that their beliefs were correct, or, at the very least, worthy of strong consideration.

So, even if the author of Genesis was "just" writing down Israel's oral traditions, this storytelling became an act of faith (and rebellion) when presented in the face of the colossal success that was the Babylonian Empire. But the author of Genesis did more than record the oral traditions; the author also included some key components of the Babylonian creation story and then turned them upside down.

---

[9] Webster, M. See resource #24 in Reference List

SCRIPTURE: *Genesis 1.1-31*

*1 In the beginning when God created the heavens and the earth, 2 the earth was a **formless void** and darkness covered the face of the deep, while a **wind** from God swept over the face of the **waters.***

3 Then God said, "Let there be light"; and there was light. 4 And God saw that the light was good; and God separated the light from the darkness. 5 God called the light Day, and the darkness he called Night. And there was evening and there was morning, the first day.

6 And God said, "Let there be a dome in the midst of the waters, and let it separate the waters from the waters." 7 So God made the dome and separated the waters that were under the dome from the waters that were above the dome. And it was so. 8 God called the dome Sky. And there was evening and there was morning, the second day.

9 And God said, "Let the waters under the sky be gathered together into one place, and let the dry land appear." And it was so. 10 God called the dry land Earth, and the waters that were gathered together he called Seas. And God saw that it was good.

11 Then God said, "Let the earth put forth vegetation: plants yielding seed, and fruit trees of every kind on earth that bear fruit with the seed in it." And it was so. 12 The earth brought forth vegetation: plants yielding seed of every kind, and trees of every kind bearing fruit with the seed in it. And God saw that it was good. 13 And there was evening and there was morning, the third day.

14 And God said, "Let there be lights in the dome of the sky to separate the day from the night; and let them be for signs and for seasons and for days and years, 15 and let them be lights in the dome of the sky to give light upon the earth." And it was so. 16 God made the two great lights-the greater light to rule the day and the lesser light to rule the night-and the stars. 17 God set them in the dome of the sky to give light upon the earth, 18 to rule over the day and over the night, and to separate the light from the darkness. And God saw that it was good. 19 And there was evening and there was morning, the fourth day.

20 And God said, "Let the waters bring forth swarms of living creatures, and let birds fly above the earth across the dome of the sky." 21 So God created the great sea monsters and every living creature that moves, of every kind, with which the waters swarm, and every winged bird of every kind. And God saw that it was good. 22 God blessed them, saying, "Be fruitful and multiply and fill the waters in the seas, and let birds multiply on the earth." 23 And there was evening and there was morning, the fifth day.

24 And God said, "Let the earth bring forth living creatures of every kind: cattle and creeping things and wild animals of the earth of every kind." And it was so. 25 God made the wild animals of the earth of every kind, and the cattle of every kind, and everything that creeps upon the ground of every kind. And God saw that it was good.

26 Then God said, "Let us make humankind in our image, according to our likeness; and let them have dominion over the fish of the sea, and over the birds of the air, and over the cattle, and over all the wild animals of the earth, and over every creeping thing that creeps upon the earth." 27 So God created humankind in his image, in the image of God he created them; male and female he created them. 28 God blessed them, and God said to them, "Be fruitful and multiply, and fill the earth and subdue it; and have dominion over the fish of the sea and over the birds of the air and over every living thing that moves upon the earth."

29 God said, "See, I have given you every plant yielding seed that is upon the face of all the earth, and every tree with seed in its fruit; you shall have them for food. 30 And to every beast of the earth, and to every bird of the air, and to everything that creeps on the earth, everything that has the breath of life, I have given every green plant for food." And it was so. 31 God saw everything that he had made, and indeed, it was very good. And there was evening and there was morning, the sixth day.

CONCEPTS

Chaos as Formless Void: Because modern lives are typically frenetic, hectic, and loud, our usage of the word "chaos" has narrowed over the years. It has always meant noisy and busy confusion, but it was also once synonymous with "the abyss." In fact, the original word, *khaos,* meant "gaping void."[10] If we combine the archaic usage of "chaos" along with our current usage of the word, then it succinctly summarizes this soupy formless void that swirls before God in the beginning: It is a shapeless *something* with *nothing* in it. It is confusion and waste. It is unordered and formless. It is chaos.

In the Bible, the wind isn't always just wind: The Hebrew word for wind is *ruach.* But, because the Hebrew language often uses one word to describe a number of concepts, *ruach* also means breath or spirit; *ruach* can even mean all three of these things (wind, breath, and spirit) at the same time.[11] Though this characteristic makes Hebrew an imprecise language, it also makes it a textured language, rich with imagery. As a result, the task of translating Hebrew into English is a difficult one, where the richness of a Hebrew passage is often "thinned-out" during translation. Genesis 1:2 is one such example. The English word choice of *wind,* here, does not nearly capture the Hebrew sense of

---

[10] Chaos. See resource #8 in Reference List
[11] Ruwach. See resource #21 in Reference List

how God's spirit and breath would have also been understood to be hovering over the chaos.

The sea as a symbol for chaos[12]: If you recall New Orleans after Hurricane Katrina or the 2011 tsunami that crashed into Japan, then it is not difficult to notice how the sea and chaos share similar characteristics of unpredictability, senselessness, and raw power. This was obvious to the storytellers in ancient times as well, where the sea was prodigiously used as a symbol for chaos.[13] The Israelites borrowed heavily from this practice and incorporated the sea as a symbol for chaos throughout their faith stories.[14] They even used the names of sea creatures from other cultures to symbolically demonstrate God's power over the chaos.[15] This symbol for chaos, then, introduced within a breath of the very beginning of Creation (*Gen. 1:2*), plays a key role in a number of the Bible stories (including the Genesis 1 creation story), and is an essential concept when interpreting the story.

---

[12] Chaos. See resource #7 in Reference List
[13] Yahweh's Conflict with the Leviathan... See resource #25 in Reference List
   Bratcher, D. See resource #5 in Reference List
[14] Enns, P. See resource #11 in Reference List
[15] Johnson, M. See resource #18 in Reference List

RUMINATIONS

I thought this book was going to be about the Bible and Christianity. Why did you begin by talking about Babylonian beliefs?

Because context is important. The Babylonian's creation story, *Enuma Elish,* like any creation story, sought to answer universal questions. What is creation made of? Where did it come from? Why is life like this?

The answer that *Enuma Elish* offers in its narrative is that creation is a product of war and destruction, a child of confusion and waste. Furthermore, *Enuma Elish* demonstrates how to deal with this chaotic creation: By fighting and then winning the conflict (whatever the conflict may be). So that's what the Babylonians did. They fought and they won.

One of the many countries that the Babylonians fought and conquered was Israel – which would suggest (quite strongly) that the Babylonians' religion/god was better and stronger than the Israelites' God. This, then, is the context and culture in which the author of Genesis was immersed. With this cultural context in mind, we can see the influence of the Babylonian beliefs when we read the Genesis creation story.

So the author of Genesis just ripped off another culture's creation story? Are you calling the author of Genesis a plagiarist?

The author of Genesis was not concerned about writing an original story, but was concerned with setting the record straight about how God created. That is why it is incredibly important to know about the *Enuma Elish* and then note the differences between it and the Genesis creation story. The author of Genesis took the conventional wisdom of the day (i.e., the *Enuma Elish* story) and turned it inside out and upside down. By doing so, the Genesis creation story offers a very different understanding of God, creation, and who we are.

For instance?

For instance, in the two stories, the material of creation is similar. In the beginning of the Genesis creation story, there was the *deep*. In the *Enuma Elish,* there was the defeated Goddess, *Tiamat…*whose name means what?

According to a previous footnote (#8), *Tiamat* is believed to be the root word for the Hebrew word for "the deep."

So the material[16] of creation (salt water/the sea/chaos) is likely meant to be understood as the same in both creation stories, but how it is dealt with and used in the two stories is quite different. *Marduk* fights the chaos. Then in a moment of triumphant rage, he hacks it apart and throws the defeated chaos all about, offering a picture of creation as violent, accidental, and random.

However, in Genesis, God does not defeat the chaos in a battle, but orders it with language.[17] Instead of creating in a

---

[16] Where the chaos originates from is a hotly debated topic among Christian theologians. Most of the arguments fall into one of two camps: The creation *ex nihilo* argument (which means "out of nothing") posits that God created the chaos (and everything else) out of nothing. The other camp argues creation *ex material*. That is: God created from pre-existing material.

The ramifications of either argument are pretty steep. If God didn't make the chaos, then who did? Maybe by an entity even more powerful than God? Or, maybe the basic material of creation is flawed (and thus the root of our daily problems)? Or, if God did create the chaos, why did God create such an unruly thing to be the building block of Creation? Surely, God is a better architect than that!?

Despite the intriguing "what ifs" such discussions raise, these arguments sidestep the intent of the story. Was the author of Genesis really trying to tell a story that supported an idea of "creation *ex nihilo*" over "creation *ex materia*" or vice versa? Or was the author of Genesis seeking to provide a written reminder that the God of Abraham, Isaac, and Jacob was more powerful than the Babylon Empire and more powerful than the chaos that the Babylonians believed was the whole of creation?

If you desire a theory about the origin of chaos that differs from the *ex nihilo* and *ex materia* arguments, consider this one: Chaos is the unformed parts of God. As God arranges and orders these parts of God's self, the result is creation / new life that cannot help but blossom with abundance and vibrancy.

burst of angry, destructive, post-war triumph, God creates thoughtfully and deliberately.

The Genesis story tells us that creation is planned. Instead of a random distribution of the spoils of war, there is intention. God creates a dome that separates the waters from the waters (in other words, separates the chaos from the chaos). Later, land is created to further separate the waters, making spaces where the water is to exist and not exist. The land is specifically described as "dry" to further drive the point home: No chaos here![18]

In Genesis 2:7, this idea of being free of the chaos is highlighted, again, when the building material of humans is described as *dust*.[19] The message cannot be clearer: Not only did

---

[17] Another aspect, and quite possibly the most notable aspect of the story that the *ex nihilo*/*ex material* argument (footnote #15) misses, is that the chaos listens and listens well to God. God says, "Go over there" and it goes over there. God says, "Let there be light" and the switch is thrown. The story isn't concerned about where the chaos originates, but the story is very clear that God has incredible command over it.

[18] Note that chaos is to be understood not as "bad" but as "misplaced." Part of creating is designating space for where the raw material will be stored. For instance, we see that the land in verse 9 further divides the remaining waters of chaos into containers called "seas." And later, in verse 20, we see that chaos, when given boundaries, sustains life, i.e., "the oceans teemed with life." With this distribution of chaos in mind, we can understand that chaos is simply in need of a specific storage space, much like dirty laundry requires a clothes hamper. There's nothing wrong with dirty laundry...until it's all over the floor. The same is true of chaos. There's nothing wrong with it until it appears where it does not belong.

[19] *...then the Lord God formed man from the dust of the ground, and breathed into his nostrils the breath of life; and the man became a living being.* (Genesis 2:7)

God design the land to be free of chaos, but God created its inhabitants to be free of the chaos as well.

But I don't understand...How can something that is made of chaos not be chaotic?

The *Enuma Elish* agrees with your question – it says that everything that is made out of chaos IS chaotic. And that's why the original fight between *Marduk* and *Tiamat* serves as a model to the Babylonians regarding how life must be lived: To continually strive against the chaos in a series of conflicts.

The Genesis story, though, says that God does not overcome the chaos, but *transforms* it, giving it form and shape. Creation is *transformed* chaos.

But that doesn't fit the world we live in today. I think the *Enuma Elish* story better explains our condition. If God is able to transform the chaos, and creation is transformed chaos, then why is life so chaotic?

The second thing the author of Genesis wants us to be aware of is God's relationship with the chaos. In the Genesis story, God's spirit hovers *above* the chaos. God's Holy Spirit is not immersed in, but separate from, the chaos.

Why does that matter?

In *Enuma Elish,* the gods are participants in the chaos; they have to fight the chaos in order to rule over it. The tools, then, that the *Enuma Elish* gods use to defeat the chaos are tools of war. According to the Babylonians, then, just like the gods fought with swords and arrows, so must Babylon meet the chaos with force. Every battle the Babylonians won further proved their belief: The gods were on their side. A similar idea still lives on today in our usage of the phrase, "Might makes right."

But the Genesis story disputes this world-view. The Genesis story says that not only were we made to live free of the chaos, but that we were made in the image of God who *also* lives free of the chaos. And, because we are made in God's image, we are then given the same tool that God uses to command the chaos.

What tool did God give us, if not a sword? What could be more powerful than a sword? Oh, I know – FIRE!

No, not fire, but *language* -- the ability to name things!

Talking? **That's not a very godly tool. Are you sure that God's great gift to us is *words*?**

Yes – and it is an amazing gift! The power of language defines and separates. The naming of things is what transforms chaos into creation.

I remain unimpressed. Maybe I would better understand with an example.

Sure! Imagine a popular county fair attended by thousands of folks, most of them belonging to families. Everybody is happy and having a good time. But, there's a problem: While a ten-year-old daughter was watching one of the attractions, she lost sight of her family. Suddenly, she was adrift in the formless and shapeless crowd.

Are you using the crowd as a symbol for chaos?

Yes. But don't worry about this daughter, because she is neither helpless nor shy. She takes a deep breath and screams, "MOOOOOOOOOOOOM!"

And just like that, hundreds of women turn and look at her. With one word, a ten-year-old took a formless and shapeless crowd and defined part of it. Not only did she define it, but that defined part of the crowd *responded* to her one word. The mothers moved in a different direction than the rest of the crowd did. Just one word did all of that!

Oh! And, if you were writing this example in the style of Genesis, you might say, "On the first yell, she called it 'Mom' and it was good."

Clever - especially since there will be a second yell. Having all these mothers looking at her hasn't solved the daughter's problem: She still can't see her family. So the daughter thinks, "That's too many moms! I'll have to use my mom's first name." So she yells a second time and of all the mothers only five share this first name and step forward.

With just two words, then, a child defined and ordered a chaotic crowd. That's how powerful language is![20]

That was good, thank you! Your example helps me see how language is a much more powerful tool than how I was thinking of it. But your example doesn't explain to me why life is so chaotic today.

Oh, but it does!

How so?

The Genesis creation story is telling us that God is so incredibly skilled at using language that God defines the chaos and thereby transforms it into creation. The story then says that we, who are made in the image of God, have at our disposal the very same tool that God wielded to order and transform the

---

[20] The other amazing thing about God using language is that, although it is a powerful tool, it also allows choice. By using language, God does not force us into obedience or relationship. Instead, the nature of language offers us the ability to say no.

chaos! But what if we were to ignore God's spirit and direction and used this tool of language all on our own without God's inspiration and instruction? What might happen?

Nothing would happen because I am not God. And neither are you. None of us are!

While "nothing" is certainly one facet of chaos (the abyss/void aspect of it), the state of the world and the lives we live say that something indeed *does* happen when we use language without God's guidance and wisdom.

Are you saying that if I speak incorrectly then I am somehow allowing the chaos to go somewhere it isn't supposed to go?!

That's a simplified explanation, but yes. Using language without God's guidance undoes the definitions that God created and then (mostly unintentionally) breaks down creation by reintroducing chaos into places where it was not designed to be.

Did you just accuse me of ruining creation!?

Actually, all of us. But don't worry, there is great hope in this accusation.

Oh really?

Remember, the *Enuma Elish* says that we, and everything else, are made of chaotic material, *Tiamat*. In other words, life is inherently chaotic because the chaos is in the *very DNA* of creation. Therefore, to survive, we have to keep fighting and doing battle with the chaos, just like *Marduk* did. According to the worldview of the Babylonians, the wolf and the lamb will never coexist; survival will always be a fight.[21]

But the Genesis creation story gives a very different picture. It tells us that the chaos is *not* built into us or creation. But then, we went and *invited* the chaos into spaces it did not belong, like our environment, lives, and bodies.

Which brings us to the most important part: *Since the chaos is invited in, then we can also **un-invite** it!* Although it would require great change in us, *it is possible* to live free of the chaos; the wolf and the lamb *can* co-exist.

I don't know. That sounds pretty far-fetched, don't you think?

Most of the Jesus stories also sound far-fetched and this is why: As long as we believe that chaos is inherent to our lives

---

[21] "...and the lion will lie down with the lamb" is more commonly uttered, but there is no Bible verse that actually uses this phrase. Isaiah 11:6 is the closest we get to it: *The wolf will live with the lamb, the leopard will lie down with the goat, the calf and the lion and the yearling together; and a little child will lead them.*

instead of a component that we invite into our lives, then our ability to live like Jesus is greatly diminished.

Jesus is the best example of what living free of the chaos looks like. He repeatedly shows us, through God's guidance and Spirit, how the chaos is ordered and transformed.

This life that is lived free of the chaos is what Jesus calls the "kingdom of God" (a.k.a., "the reign of God" – as mentioned in the Introduction). Jesus goes on to say that the kingdom of God is "near" and "at hand."

When he tells his disciples to follow him, he's telling them (and by extension, us) that they, too, can learn to live God's way, the way that is free of the chaos. It isn't easy, but it *is* possible.

Whoa! So, like, all of the mysteries of life are explained right here, in the first chapter of Genesis!?

Not quite. But, as we can see, the importance of Genesis 1 does not come from unique plot lines or character development. Instead, it is the relationship between God and chaos that makes Genesis 1 a stunning counter-cultural message, not just then, but for today, too.

Genesis brilliantly reminds the Israelites that goodness is inherent in God's design of creation. Goodness, joy, excitement, peace, order and more exist because that is how God designed creation and humankind. It is the chaos, then, that is the anomaly, not goodness.

Over 2500 years later, the Genesis creation story still holds this same pertinent message for us. It reminds us that we are not made to fight, sink into, or wallow in the chaos. Instead, we are to turn to the God who makes a way for us through the chaos and invites us to live free of it.

Suggested Outline for
CLASS DISCUSSION

1. **Opening Prayer** (1 to 2 minutes) – Facilitator or group member says a prayer aloud at the agreed-upon starting time of the class.

2. **Opening Question** (10 minutes) – Facilitator or group member asks the chapter's opening question for the group to discuss/share: *Birth stories – be they stories of life, love, pursuit, or work – strongly shape how we live, love, pursue, and work. If you are willing, share (somewhat briefly) a beginnings story with the group. For example: The birth of a child; how you met your spouse; how you got the job/career you are currently in; how you received a pet; how you joined the church you are attending, etc.*

3. **Read the chapter's scripture passage**

4. **Discussion** (30 to 35 minutes) – Facilitator asks the group one of the following questions and the group responds. In theory, each question is meant to take about 5 minutes of discussion, but in reality some questions will elicit more conversation and sharing than other questions:

   a) Share with the group one or two points in the Context, Scripture Reading, Concepts, and Ruminations sections that you appreciated, disagreed with, struggled to accept or didn't understand.

b) We just finished reading a chapter that explores two stories about what creation is made of (chaos). What do *you* think creation is made of??

c) *Follow-up to Question B:* How do you think your answer (about the building material of creation) informs your understanding of the nature of life, who God is, and what God offers?

d) In the Ruminations section, there is some discussion about God using the tool of language to define the chaos and transform it into creation. What tools, if any, have you typically thought of God using and to what effect?

e) *Follow-up to Question D:* Do you think it was a good choice by God to share the gift of language with us/humans?

f) One of the conclusions in the *Ruminations* section is that the presence of chaos in our lives is not a foregone conclusion. Since it was invited in, it can also be invited to leave. What do you think about that idea?

g) *Follow-up to Question F:* The *Ruminations* section ends by reiterating a message from the Genesis story that we are not made to live in or wallow in chaos. In what ways do you experience chaos that you would like to not experience anymore?

5. **Discuss details for next class** (e.g., when it will happen and what chapter to read in preparation)

6. **Closing Prayer** (3 to 7 minutes) – Facilitator opens the prayer and then ceases his/her out loud praying to allow members of the group to pray out loud/silently for whatever comes to mind. Facilitator then closes the prayer.

2. The Flood

the inclination of hearts, corruption & inebriation

◻ ▪ ◻ ◻ ◻ ◻

CONTEXT

As with the creation story, the Noah story (i.e., the flood story) is not unique to the Israelites. Other ancient civilizations (like the Sumerians and Babylonians) also told flood stories. This overlap of stories has led to a reasonable theory that some sort of flood did indeed occur, most likely of staggering proportions, though not of the entire planet.[22]

In Genesis, the Noah/flood story takes place at the end of a disturbing sequence of stories. After God created and saw that "It was very good," Adam and Eve are quick to ignore the reign of God and function as their own gods – which leads to their eviction from the Garden of Eden. A number of years after their eviction, Cain (one of their sons) murders another of their sons, Abel.

---

[22] How should we... See resource #15 in Reference List
Isaak, M. See resource #16 in Reference List

One might think that sons killing each other would serve as a strong-enough indicator that life lived without God was not the better choice; one might also think that humankind would be quick to recognize its error and return God to God's rightful place as our internal sovereign. But, as we see at the start of the Noah story, such thinking was far from the norm.

Scripture: *Genesis 6:5-22*

5 *The Lord saw that the wickedness of humankind was great in the earth, and that every inclination of the thoughts of their hearts was only **evil** continually. 6 And the Lord was sorry that he had made humankind on the earth, and it grieved him to his heart. 7 So the Lord said, "I will blot out from the earth the human beings I have created-people together with animals and creeping things and birds of the air, for I am sorry that I have made them."*

8 *But Noah found favor in the sight of the Lord. 9 Noah was a **righteous** man, blameless in his generation; Noah walked with God. 10 And Noah had three sons, Shem, Ham, and Japheth. 11 Now the earth was **corrupt** in God's sight, and the earth was filled with violence. 12 And God saw that the earth was corrupt; for all flesh had corrupted its ways upon the earth. 13 And God said to Noah, "I have determined to make an end of all flesh, for the earth is filled with violence because of*

them; now I am going to destroy them along with the earth. *14 Make yourself an ark of cypress wood; make rooms in the ark, and cover it inside and out with pitch. 15 This is how you are to make it: the length of the ark three hundred cubits, its width fifty cubits, and its height thirty cubits. 16 Make a roof for the ark, and finish it to a cubit above; and put the door of the ark in its side; make it with lower, second, and third decks. 17 For my part, I am going to bring a flood of waters on the earth, to destroy from under heaven all flesh in which is the breath of life; everything that is on the earth shall die. 18 But I will establish my covenant with you; and you shall come into the ark, you, your sons, your wife, and your sons' wives with you. 19 And of every living thing, of all flesh, you shall bring two of every kind into the ark, to keep them alive with you; they shall be male and female. 20 Of the birds according to their kinds, and of the animals according to their kinds, of every creeping thing of the ground according to its kind, two of every kind shall come in to you, to keep them alive. 21 Also take with you every kind of food that is eaten, and store it up; and it shall serve as food for you and for them." 22 Noah did this; he did all that God commanded him.*

CONCEPTS

How we think about "Evil": *"...every inclination of the thoughts of their hearts was only evil continually..."* We often associate evil with morally reprehensible behavior, sometimes even giving credit to an evil overlord (often called the "Devil" or "Satan") who does battle with God and can somehow influence our choices. But when we base the word "evil" on observable actions, then that puts us in the position of having to judge/determine which actions are evil. This position mirrors Adam and Eve's original sin: Humans deciding what was right and wrong on their own instead of seeking and trusting God's reign.

In the Noah story, though, the evil that is noted is seen through God's eyes, not a person's eyes. Furthermore, God observes evil residing *inside* the people: "Every inclination of the **thoughts** of their **hearts** was only evil" (emphasis added). This distinction of evil as an internal condition instead of an external action is a narrower definition of the word than we usually give it. The Noah story also gives us a word to describe the observable (i.e. external) action that, nowadays, we usually refer to as "evil." See the "Corruption" entry for more information.

Noah was a righteous man: *"Noah was a righteous man, blameless in his generation; Noah walked with God."* Righteousness can be defined as "right relationship with God." Righteousness, like evil, refers not to observable actions, but to the internal focus of our hearts and minds (that then becomes observable in our decisions and actions). It is Noah's choice to let God define and determine his life's choices that gives him the status of "righteous." And, because Noah is walking God's way, then he (and those who are close to him) can see and travel God's offered path through the chaos.

Corruption in the Noah story is equivalent to what we now call "Evil.": *"And God saw that the earth was **corrupt**; for all flesh had corrupted its ways upon the earth."* The Noah story uses the word, "corrupt," in the way that we usually use the word, "evil." When humans are so internally preoccupied that they cannot/will not pay attention to God, then that "evil" condition results in our imperfect impersonation of playing God; we continue to use language, but without God's guidance or wisdom, we misuse it. The result of this misuse is an observable undoing (i.e. a corruption) of God's good creation.[23]

---

[23] There are two other words that we think work just as well as corruption, but are not used in the Noah story, thus relegating these sentences to footnote status: *Dissolution* and *Decay*. Dissolution would be an especially useful word, since it describes what happens to a material when placed in certain liquids (like water) – it dissolves. In other words, the water (a.k.a. *chaos*) undoes the object. Decay offers the same idea but along the lines of life and death – a life without God is unsustainable and ultimately loses its form.

RUMINATIONS

The teaching of the Noah story is often relegated to the Sunday school classrooms of our youngest children, where they learn of the animals going into the ark.

I remember how this story fascinated me when I was younger. How did Noah keep the predators from eating the prey? Why did Noah save the mosquito? What kind of waste management system was implemented?

It is good to ask and talk about questions like these, especially with children, but this is also why the story should be revisited when we are adults, because there is so much more to discuss.

You're telling me! How about God being a mass-murderer!? We certainly didn't cover that aspect of the story in Sunday school!

Indeed, some of God's actions in this story are disturbing. Furthermore, God's apparent heavy-handedness obscures the humans' complicity in their own demise.

But I don't see any complicity. I see a very severe punishment that does not seem to fit the crime.

In chapter 1, we discussed how the cultural context of the author influenced the telling of the creation story. In the Noah story, we see the author's contextual and cultural theology of God's supreme sovereignty bleed into the writing as well.

What do you mean?

When Genesis was written, there was an understanding about God (a theology) that *everything* that happened in the world was God's doing. If it rained and crops grew, that was God's doing. If there was drought and the crops didn't grow, that was God's doing. If your child lived, that was God's doing. If your child died, that was God's doing.

As in, "The Lord giveth and the Lord taketh away"?

Exactly. Regardless of whether something was good or bad, right or wrong, exciting or scary, it all emanated from God. In this case, with the Noah story, that includes assigning responsibility for the flood to God.

But doesn't this lead to some pretty obvious contradictions in the story? God wants to kill all the people and animals, but at the very same time, God wants to save Noah, Noah's family, and a bunch of their pets! It's almost like God was for creation before God was against it. Doesn't the

author care that the left hand of God doesn't know what the right hand of God is doing?

Obviously, these contradictions did not concern the author of Genesis. But our *own* cultural sensibilities are certainly concerned about these contradictions. Unfortunately, these sensibilities only add another layer of noise between our reading of the story and our comprehension of it, which is why a new telling of the story might be a helpful endeavor.

Are you saying you want to retell the Noah story?

Yes. What do you think about that?

I'm definitely curious...Go for it!

Once upon a time, God made a beautiful garden for humans to live in and enjoy. It was an incredibly large, complex, and beautiful place. The people liked it a lot. One thing they especially enjoyed was that they could participate in the upkeep and management of the garden. But because it was so large and complex, the people simply could not care for it all by themselves. They needed God's help and direction to properly care for the garden. But the humans were often distracted by their life in the garden. So distracted, in fact, that they mostly forgot to ask for God's help and direction.

This forgetting about God led the humans to make mistakes while they cared for the garden. They over-watered some of the land and under-watered other parts of the land. They used resources in one area of the garden that should've been used in another area of the garden. This misuse of resources caused the people to then argue about who should receive what and why they should receive it. These arguments often ended in fights. The fighting created more distractions and more arguments which then led to more problems and more fighting. This went on and on until the humans were so completely overwhelmed with the state of their garden and their life in the garden that they had completely forgotten about God. Such behavior and events even led many to believe that God did not exist.

God could see that disaster was imminent and was disgusted by the damage the people had done to the very good Garden. But despite God's disgust, God was still willing to work with any human who might listen. It turns out that there was one inhabitant in the garden who kept seeking God's wisdom and direction. His name was Noah. So God shared a plan with Noah that would save Noah and the most important aspects of the garden from the impending disaster that the people were creating for themselves. Because Noah listened to and was obedient to God, then he, his family, and the most important plants and animals from the garden were saved when disaster struck.

Your retelling certainly shifts the blame without lessening God's displeasure. And, I can see what you meant, then, about the original story "obscuring the humans' complicity in their

own demise." But what does this story have to do with us right here, right now?

The Noah story helps us think about how we (inadvertently) invite the chaos into our lives, the effects we experience when we invite the chaos in, and what options are available to us with God once we realize that we've made this mistake and want to correct it.

Can you say more about how I or others invite chaos into life?

By having evil thoughts —

But I'm not wicked or evil or bad! I might make a mistake here or there, and I've been known to get a little cranky, but I don't *kill* people. I don't steal things. All in all, I'm a pretty good person. I go to worship services, I stop at crosswalks, I help neighbors with yard work, I vote, I pay my taxes – I even tip at 20% or higher!

But those are things that you *do*. The Noah story in verse 5 defines "evil" differently than how you are.

God isn't looking at the people's actions. God is looking at the inclination of the people's thoughts and hearts, at their interior lives. And the inclination of the people's hearts and minds is evil – or in other words – focused somewhere other than on God.

I don't see how you understand the story to specifically define evil as "focused somewhere other than on God."

If we compare the descriptions of the internal state of Noah and his neighbors, we can see that the difference is that Noah focuses his attention on God and his neighbors do not.

In addition to that comparison, we can add some helpful parallels from a Jesus story. After Jesus tells his disciples that he's going to be arrested, killed, and then resurrected, Peter takes Jesus aside and rebukes him, saying, "God forbid it, Lord! This must never happen to you." This is an expression of care from Peter. But what is Jesus' response? He tells Peter, "Get behind me, Satan! You are setting your mind not on divine things but on human things."[24]

Was Jesus having a bad day? That seems like a bit of an over-reaction.

Agreed. Peter's actions certainly do not appear to be evil; he's simply expressing care for his rabbi! But Jesus' response is about the inclination of Peter's mind. Jesus knows that Peter is setting his mind on human things, instead of divine things.

---

[24] Matthew 16:22-23

Jesus' understanding of Peter's actions is very similar to how evil is being understood in the Noah story.

But I don't like that at all! Basically, you're saying that if I stop to smell the roses or read a book for a half-hour and don't think about God while I do it, then I'm evil! That is an *unrealistic* expectation!

Do not dismiss the word "continually" that is in verse 5. The people were *continually* paying attention to the book, to the roses, and to everything else except for God. The point is that they never *stopped* paying attention to the other things.

Okay, but this really challenges how I've understood evil. For instance, I've always believed that there were good people who fought against evil people. But you can't really fight evil if it is a lack of spiritual focus. How *do* you fight against a lack of spiritual focus?

Before we discuss "fighting," let's introduce the concept of corruption, since it makes an appearance in verse 11.

Yeah, that "corruption of flesh" phrase is weird. What does it mean?

In verse 5, God sees evil inside the people. But by verse 11, God is noticing something else: Corruption. What makes corruption different from evil is that corruption is *visible* in the physical world. The story says it is first seen in the flesh, then in the earth, and finally in violence (i.e., our interactions with each other and with the environment/earth).

What's being observed, then, is a progression starting with continually evil thoughts that results in a corrupted world. This progression is comparable to the development of a virus: Thoughts that preclude God reach a critical mass (i.e., an infection), which corrupt the flesh and the earth (i.e., fever, congestion), and eventually result in violence (i.e., coughing, shivering, vomiting).

But when we are sick, don't we "treat the symptoms?" Isn't that also how we should fight evil? By treating the symptom of corruption?

No.

No!? Then what do we fight?

Nothing.

Nothing?

The siren call of chaos is, "Manage me." The temptation is to fight it and conquer it, just like *Marduk* defeated *Tiamat*. But whenever we heed that temptation, that siren call, all we actually achieve is the spreading of the chaos, just like *Marduk* did: He cut up the chaos (*Tiamat*) and spread it around.

The more we attempt to defeat the chaos, the more chaos we spread about us. And, if we continue upon this path of *Marduk*, eventually, we find ourselves fully submersed in chaos.

So basically you're saying we should just "let go and let God?"

Yes and no. To "let go and let God" *should* mean seeking God's guidance and choosing to move along the path that God reveals to us (i.e., "walk with God" like Noah did). The reason we would choose to seek God's guidance is because we're willing to admit that we cannot determine or correctly identify the (often) counter-intuitive decisions needed to stay free of chaos. To admit this inability would certainly be a "letting go."

However, people often use the phrase "let go and let God" to mean, "I'm going to live my life as I want and God will take care of the rest." This approach, though, avoids recognition of how our own actions helped undo creation in the first place – which is the approach that Noah's neighbors modeled ("every inclination of the thoughts of their hearts was only evil continually"). Not paying attention to how God calls us to function differently is not "letting go and letting God."

So if Noah had just kept going his own way, things would not have turned out very well for him. But because he let go of his own way and chose God's way, then he was able to avoid the temptation of managing the chaos.

Exactly!

You know, the more we talk about it and the more I think about it, the more difficult Noah's choice seems. Noah had *a lot* to do because of God. Listening for and obeying God completely changed his life.

Yes. For Noah, there was a great amount of work and time that went into his ark-building project without any guarantee that his work would have value. Viewed from an in-the-moment perspective, Noah's decision to follow God's way was incredibly illogical. Foolish, even. It made no sense. Noah probably received grief from his family and perhaps derision from his neighbors. Because the characters in the Noah story were *living* the story, they could not know the *end* of the story, and without knowing the end of the story, Noah's actions made no sense.

But because *we* know how the story ends, then we can see how Noah's decision to let God reign in his life was an impressive decision – and the best one he could have made. That decision changed his life and then saved his life.

We also see that although God's overall instruction to Noah seemed irrational ("Build a boat in your backyard, far away from any water" – not verbatim, by the way), God's step-by-step instructions to Noah about the actual boat were logical, practical, and clear (*vv.* 15-16). In addition, God gave Noah enough time, instruction, and opportunity to finish the project.

Are you suggesting that a decision to seek first God's kingdom will result in a better life, but at the same time will not necessarily be considered logical by others, rewarded in the short-term, nor treated with respect by my family and neighbors?

Yes, that is a likely outcome. If we refer to the Jesus story mentioned previously, Peter's response to Jesus seeking God's way through the chaos was very similar: "This is CRAZY! Don't do it!" But because Jesus listened to God instead of Peter, then what followed was the Resurrection. Again, because we know the end of the story, Jesus' actions do not seem super-crazy. But, in the moment to Peter and the other disciples, Jesus' decisions seemed foolish.

The real-world experience of living in the reign of God is that we *cannot* see how our story ends. Often, the path that God will show us will appear counter-intuitive to achieving how we *think* the story will end.

In the short-term, letting God reign in our lives is the illogical, harder, less-rewarding choice. The temptation, then, as always, is to heed chaos' call of "Manage me." It will beckon and tease and say, "What God is calling you to do is crazy. It won't work. *You* know the better way to manage me. *You* know exactly what needs to be done."

Hey! I *know* that voice!

Don't we all? But don't listen to that voice! Don't stage an internal coup d'état and overthrow God's reign from your life. Instead, remember Noah and how he walked with God. And, remember that choosing God's way is also better for those who are with us.

Are you referring to Noah's wife and immediate family?

Yes. It is not just Noah who found himself above the chaos when the rain came down and the floods came up. The benefit of God's reign extended to Noah's wife, his sons, their families and all of the animals who came along for the ride.

Since you just brought them up, can you please say something...ANYTHING...about the animals?

The animal component of the story certainly seems fanciful, but it reminds us that following the path that God reveals to us also resonates with God's creation. Earlier in the story, the earth is observed as corrupted and because of it, the water levels rise (i.e., nature responds unfavorably). But because Noah follows God's way and instructions, then the animals flock to him (i.e., nature responds favorably).

Oh, that's good. I like that! But, I have one more question about this story. Noah is obedient and all of the corrupted behavior and evil thoughts are washed away by the flood. This means we live in a post-flood world. Shouldn't that also mean that the chaos is gone? And yet, I still see lots of chaos. Why isn't the world redeemed?

Because the chaos and the temptation to manage it is always available. As for Noah, it seems that he was better able to seek God in the stirred-up version of chaos. But what we see later in the story is that after the flood recedes and Noah disembarks from the ark, he experiences the flip-side of chaos: The void. The meaningless waste. The abyss.

In the swirling storm of chaos, when nothing made sense, when all his neighbors were out-of-control, Noah was able to hold tightly to God. But once the wind died down, once the storm left its trail of disaster, Noah did not adhere as closely in his relationship with God.

Wait! What are you talking about? What happened!?

After the flood, and after Noah disembarks from the ark, Noah gets drunk. And while he's inebriated (overwhelmed by a different type of liquid), something happens between him and his sons, specifically with Ham.[25]

Then, the next day, Noah curses Ham for the actions of the previous night. And that's all we hear about it. However, in following Old Testament stories, "Ham" becomes a shorthand explanation of where Israel's enemies originated. For example, Egypt, which we'll talk about in the next chapter, plays prominently in Israel's oppression and is occasionally referred to as "the land of Ham."[26] Also, Nimrod, a grandson of Ham, is considered the father of the Babylonians – another oppressor of Israel.[27]

So even as Noah demonstrates why letting God reign in our lives is advantageous, Noah also serves as the perfect example of how just a little bit of chaos, even when it appears to have receded from our lives, can be deadly.

---

[25] Genesis 9:20-25
[26] Egypt as the "land of Ham": Psalms 78:51; 105:23; 106:22
[27] Genesis 10:6-10

Suggested Outline for
CLASS DISCUSSION

1. **Opening Prayer** (1 to 2 minutes) – Facilitator or group member says a prayer aloud at the agreed-upon starting time of the class.

2. **Opening Question** (10 minutes) – Facilitator or group member asks the chapter's opening question for the group to discuss/share: *What is something you would like to do, but are too embarrassed or too uncomfortable to do?*

3. **Read the chapter's scripture passage.** Also consider reading the re-telling of the Noah story as told in the Ruminations section

4. **Discussion** (30 to 35 minutes) – Facilitator asks the group one of the following questions and the group responds. In theory, each question is meant to take about 5 minutes of discussion, but in reality some questions will elicit more conversation and sharing than other questions:

   a) Share with the group one or two points in the Context, Scripture Reading, Concepts, and Ruminations sections that you appreciated, disagreed with, struggled to accept or didn't understand.

b) Most of us tend to not talk about trying to be "righteous," but we might talk about how we try to be "a good person." In what ways do you try to be a good person?

c) *Follow-up question to Question B:* Using the understanding of the word "righteous" as used in the Noah story (ways we try to keep our mind and heart on God), in what ways do you think trying to be a "righteous" person differs from trying to be a "good" person?

d) Noah seemed better at knowing his need of God when he was in the turbulent form of chaos than when he was in the void form of chaos. What form of chaos (the chaotic storm or the void) unsettles you the most? What form of chaos is more likely to have you seeking God's guidance?

e) Conversely, what form of chaos are you most comfortable in? In what type of situation are you most tempted to "overthrow" God as the top authority in your life and start making your own decisions?

f) Now that you've identified moments when you are most likely to overthrow God to command the chaos yourself, what reminders can you use to help yourself remember to pray and invite God into the chaos to re-establish God's reign in that time and place?

5. **Discuss details for next class** (e.g., when it will happen and what chapter to read in preparation)

6. **Closing Prayer** (3 to 7 minutes) – Facilitator opens the prayer and then ceases his/her out loud praying to allow members of the group to pray out loud/silently for whatever comes to mind. Facilitator then closes the prayer.

3. Crossing the Red Sea

mitsrayim, the Titanic & God's grace

❑ ❑ ■ ❑ ❑ ❑

CONTEXT

This chapter's scripture passage describes part of the emancipation of the Israelite people from Egypt.

The story of the Israelites' enslavement by the Egyptians begins with Jacob (renamed as "Israel") and his twelve sons. Of those sons, Joseph was Jacob's favorite. He showered Joseph with gifts, most notably, a robe. Joseph's brothers, due to a combination of jealousy and annoyance, did not have similar affection for Joseph and eventually sold Joseph to Egyptian slave traders (unbeknownst to their father).

Joseph's enslavement and imprisonment in Egypt ended when Joseph, with God's help, interpreted a recurring dream of Pharaoh's. When Joseph informed Pharaoh that his dream foretold of seven abundant crop years followed by seven years of famine, Joseph also proposed storing food during the good years to help prepare for the lean years. Pharaoh agreed and assigned Joseph to oversee the task. By the time the famine arrived, Egypt was well-stocked and its surplus of food attracted people from the surrounding lands, including Joseph's brothers. Joseph and his brothers eventually reconciled during those famine years, which led to Jacob (a.k.a., Israel) and his sons moving to Egypt.

Despite Joseph's role in helping Egypt, the Egyptians did not honor Joseph's family (the Israelites) as the years passed. During the next 400 years, the Egyptians slowly enslaved the Israelites based on a growing concern that the Israelites were an internal threat to Egypt as they grew in strength and numbers. This slow process of enslavement may help explain the Hebrew name for Egypt, *mitsrayim*, which means "a narrow, constricted place."

By the time Moses was born, Egypt's oppression of the Israelites was complete. To keep the Israelites weak, Egypt was drowning baby Israelite boys (a brutal, but effective way to limit a people's strength). Moses escaped this fate because his mother set him above the water in a floating basket. This choice proved especially wise after an Egyptian princess found him there and adopted him.

By the time God called Moses to set the Israelites free, Moses was living in the wilderness, forty years removed from his days of royalty. Though reluctant, Moses obeyed God's directions to return to Egypt and instruct Pharaoh to release the Israelites. But Pharaoh refused. A painful process of disengaging the Israelites from the Egyptians then ensued in the form of ten increasingly disruptive and destructive plagues.

The final plague was the death of the eldest son in each household. Households marked by a lamb's blood on the doorway, however, were passed over by God's angel of death (this is remembered as "Passover" since the appropriately marked households were "passed over"). In the resulting confusion and grief, Pharaoh (finally!) released the Israelites. But soon after their departure, Pharaoh changed his mind and gave chase to recapture his cheap labor force. It is at this point in the story where the following scripture passage begins.

Scripture: *Exodus 14:9-16; 21-28*

*9 The Egyptians—all Pharaoh's horses and chariots, horsemen and troops—pursued the Israelites and overtook them as they camped by the sea near Pi Hahiroth, opposite Baal Zephon. 10 As Pharaoh approached, the Israelites looked up, and there were the Egyptians, marching after them. They were terrified and cried out to the LORD. 11 They said to Moses, "Was it because there were no graves in **Egypt** that you brought us to the desert to die? What have you done to us by* *bringing us out of Egypt? 12 Didn't we say to you in Egypt, 'Leave us alone; let us serve the Egyptians'? It would have been better for us to serve the Egyptians than to die in the desert!" 13 Moses answered the people, "Do not be afraid. Stand firm and you will see the deliverance the LORD will bring you today. The Egyptians you see today you will never see again. 14 The LORD will fight for you; you need only to be still." 15 Then the LORD said to Moses, "Why are you crying out to me? Tell the Israelites to move on. 16 Raise your staff and stretch out your hand over the sea to divide the water so that the Israelites can go through the sea on dry ground."*

21 Then Moses stretched out his hand over the sea, and all that night the LORD drove the sea back with a strong east wind and turned it into dry land. The waters were divided, 22 and the Israelites went through the sea on dry ground, with a wall of water on their right and on their left. 23 The Egyptians pursued them, and all Pharaoh's horses and chariots and horsemen followed them into the sea. 24 During the last watch of the night the LORD looked down from the pillar of fire and cloud at the Egyptian army and threw it into confusion. 25 He made the wheels of their chariots come off so that they had difficulty driving. And the Egyptians said, "Let's get away from the Israelites! The LORD is fighting for them against Egypt." 26 Then the LORD said to Moses, "Stretch out your hand over the sea so that the waters may flow back over the Egyptians and their chariots and horsemen." 27 Moses stretched out his hand over the sea, and at daybreak the sea went back to its place. The Egyptians were fleeing toward it, and the LORD swept them into the sea. 28 The water flowed back and covered the chariots and horsemen—the entire army of Pharaoh that had followed the Israelites into the sea. Not one of them survived.

CONCEPTS

Egypt as *mitsrayim*: The Hebrew word for Egypt is *mitsrayim*. Its origins are unknown. Some say it derives from *metzeir* which translates as "to border," "to shut," and "to limit."[28] Others think the root word for *mitsrayim* is *tsar* (or *tzar*) which usually means "narrow" or "adversary."[29] Scholars *do* agree that the name of *mitsrayim* is meant to connote narrowness, stress, and opposition. In short, oppression.

Displacement: When something is moved from its original position and placed elsewhere, it can be described as "displaced." From a scientific perspective, *displacement* refers to the amount/volume of solution (such as water) that an object displaces when placed in the solution. Both understandings of the word will be helpful as we discuss how *mitsrayim* attempts to manage chaos.

---

[28] Young, E. See resource #26 in Reference List
[29] *Tsar*. (Brown-Driver-Briggs) See resource #23 in Reference List

RUMINATIONS

If you live in or have visited the northern Pacific coast, you may have seen a sight that is familiar to residents near Rialto Beach, WA. There, standing watch in the surf, are large, isolated outcroppings of rock called "sea stacks." These sea stacks are the stubborn remnants of a shoreline that once existed a number of miles farther west. But over the millennia, the sea has whittled away the surrounding rock and land, pushing the shoreline east and leaving the sea stacks as a lone memorial to the land that once was.

Along this same shoreline, the beach is littered with massive fir and hemlock tree trunks that have washed ashore. Alarmingly, signs at the entrance to the beach warn visitors to stay clear of these logs at high tide because the waves can toss them even farther inland, causing injury or death in the process.

That sounds both scary and impressive!

Even without such naked displays of power, it is not surprising that people in the ancient world, including the Israelites, would choose to use the sea as a symbol for chaos. Since the beginning of time, people have observed the power of waves and storms eroding the land, capsizing ships, and easily tossing about heavy objects.

But that hasn't stopped us from building boats and braving the seas.

Very true. Nor has the power of chaos kept us from attempting to control it in our daily lives. One "character" in this chapter's story, Egypt, and by extension, Pharaoh, represents our conventional approach of trying to tame the chaos without God's help. This conventional approach has many implementations and can go by many names: Empire, Kingdom, Nation, Regime, Hierarchy, Institution, Government, Corporation, Administration, Economy, Bureaucracy, etc. For the rest of the book, then, we will appropriate the Hebrew name for Egypt, *mitsrayim*, and use it to refer to the life that we build on our own without God.

Why?

For some of us, the aforementioned institutions have some positive associations to them. This can make it difficult to remember that their true intent is to tame the chaos without God's help. By using the term *mitsrayim*, we are, hopefully, cutting the association with those more positive aspects which will help us better remember their true intent and cost.

And what is *mitsrayim's* "true intent?"

In chapter 1, we discussed how God uses language to define the chaos, thereby transforming the chaos into creation. In chapters 1 and 2, we discussed how we've received this same gift of language, but often use it without God's guidance and wisdom (which happens when we are continually focusing our hearts and minds on human things, not divine things), thereby undoing God's good creation with our words. The result is the flooding of chaos into places where it was not meant to be.

Mitsrayim, then, is how our communities, cultures, and countries attempt to manage the chaos once it is present. But, when we manage the chaos on our own, then we cannot do like God does; we cannot transform the chaos into creation. We cannot change it. We cannot transform it. And, we cannot get rid of it. We can only displace it.

Where does the chaos go when we displace it?

In general, the empire/*mitsrayim* strategy is to force or manipulate the weaker, marginalized, and impoverished segments of the population to act as a buffer between its preferred citizens and the chaos.

Egypt's enslavement of the Israelites and the resulting infanticide of the Israelite babies is one example of how one grouping of humanity can be forced to "pay" for another group's freedom from the chaos.

When you mentioned the cost of *mitsrayim* a few paragraphs ago is this what you were referring to? Are you saying that *mitsrayim* sacrifices babies as a form of payment to manage the chaos?

Yes, but not just babies. For a (relatively) recent example, consider *The Titanic*, the failed ocean-liner. The rooms of the second- and third-class cabins were located lower in the ship. After the ship hit the iceberg, had the fail-safes worked correctly, the lower floors would have been sealed, keeping the water from further flooding the ship. While this would have been helpful to the first-class passengers and the ship as a whole, it also would have sacrificed the lives of the lower-class passengers in the process.[30]

In the Exodus story, we see a similar dynamic – the citizens of Egypt (i.e., the first-class passengers) had transferred their own share of the chaos onto the shoulders of the Israelites (i.e., the third-class passengers). The killing of Israelite babies was an extension of this dynamic.

As I think about this, I find myself getting angry. This is *not* right! But, at the same time, doesn't it seem like this type of

---

[30] Although the fail-safes did not work, the actual survivor numbers of *The Titanic* still greatly favored the higher classes: Only 3% of first-class women died compared to 54% of third-class women. 67% of first-class men lost their lives compared to 92% of second-class men and 84% of third-class men. (Anesi, C. See resource #2 in Reference List)

oppression needs a large majority of the people to agree to the implementation of the *mitsrayim*? I mean, all the blame can't be pinned on Egypt, can it? The Israelites must've somehow been at fault for allowing the Egyptians to do this, right?

Your observation skates dangerously close to the "blame the victim" zone. But, the Exodus narrative does reveal an Israelite attachment to their enslaved way of life.

For instance, when Moses was a prince in Egypt, the Israelites did not support him when he killed an Egyptian slave driver. This was a rash and indefensible action by Moses, most likely driven by guilt, but certainly a sign of support from Moses towards the Israelites. Instead of being appreciative, though, the Israelites threatened to tell on him (Exodus 2:14), which led to Moses fleeing the region and becoming a goat herder. Forty years later, when he returned with God's demand that Pharaoh release the Israelites, Pharaoh's response was to increase labor demands on the Israelites. The Israelites then told Moses to stop demanding their release because he was only making things worse (Exodus 5:21). Then, in this chapter's scripture story, as the Egyptian army descends upon the Israelites, the Israelites turn on Moses again (in verse 12), "Didn't we say to you in Egypt, 'Leave us alone; let us serve the Egyptians'?"

This is exactly my point – I do *not* understand why the Israelites give in so easily to the Egyptians. What is wrong with them!?

The same thing that is "wrong" with all of us – they were trusting in something other than God to save them from the chaos. We can hear this lack of trust in God when they say to Moses, "Were there not enough graves in Egypt that you brought us out here to die?" In other words, the Israelites doubted that God could deal with the chaos any better than the *mitsrayim* could. And, they feared that this new deviation from the norm was stirring the waters of chaos to the point of total destruction.

So you're saying the only two options the Israelites knew were to either fight the *mitsrayim* or be enslaved by the *mitsrayim*? And of those two options, being enslaved seemed like the better option?

Yes, except the situation was even worse at this point in the story. The Israelites had trusted God just enough to forgo the protection of the *mitsrayim.* Because of their audacity to (hesitantly) try a third option (i.e., trust God and God's way) and leave the *mitsrayim*, the armies of the *mitsrayim* were preparing to punish them and force them back into the system.

Unfortunately, the only exit for the Israelites was blocked by the sea. It was an impossible situation with no obvious solution.

It's almost like they were stuck between the devil and the deep blue sea!

This predicament – this choice between chaos and *mitsrayim* – often ensnares us as well. This is why it is important to note what the Israelites did next.

You mean the part where they walked between walls of water?

No.

Walking between walls of water isn't something to pay attention to?

Walking between the walls of water is a great *result*. But what we want to look at is what *caused* the water to separate in the first place.

Well, duh. God did it.

But there's more to it than that. God did not act alone in this story. This is important to note because one of the main premises of this chapter and book is that the one true way to navigate free of the chaos is by *participating* in the reign of God. It is not that

God magically parted the water so that the Israelites could escape that is so amazing (even though it is amazing), but that, when in crisis, the Israelites did two things that invited God into their escape from the *mitsrayim* and chaos.

1. They cried out to the Lord (*vv.* 10)
2. They listened for and then acted upon God's direction(s).

However, the Israelites were not very practiced at listening to God which is why it was a good thing that Moses was with them. When the Israelites cried out to God, it was Moses who reminded them that they must also listen for a response. He did this by telling them to trust God and be still (*vv.* 13).

That seems a little hard to believe.

What part seems hard to believe?

The "being still" part.

Why?

Because in this situation, time is precious! Every moment counts! The Israelites need to be doing something – *anything* – to escape!

Which is pretty much how we feel in any pressure-filled situation, right? We *must act* before it is too late – at least that's what we think. And that's why this moment is so crucial to note. To be aware of God's unique and capable approach to dealing with the chaos, we have to listen for and then respond to God's leading. It *is* a little hard to believe that the Israelites chose to hold still in a moment of crisis, but their act of being still enabled Moses to hear God's directions regarding what to do next.

Which means that NOW they can walk between the walls of water?!

Not yet. First, there is something Moses must do because God does not act until Moses acts. Only when Moses raised his staff and stretched his hand over the water, did the waters part. In other words, there is a participatory relationship between God's power and Moses' actions.

Why pay attention to this?

Although the reign of God is the better way to live, God does not force it upon us. We must willingly choose to listen for and then participate in God's directions. It was because of Moses' obedience and willful participation in the reign of God that the Israelite people were finally able to—

WALK BETWEEN WALLS OF WATER!?!

Yes, walk between walls of water! Notice, though, that the author is excited about something more than just the parting of the Red Sea.

How can you tell the author is "excited"?

Repetition in the Bible is often a sign of emphasis. Think of it like Biblical highlighter. And what gets repeated in three different places in this part of the story is that the ground between the walls of water was dry (*vv.* 15, 21 & 22); the Israelites didn't cross through muddy sand or a shallow, marshy land – they crossed on dry land.[31] When God provides a way through the chaos, it is a way that is free of the chaos.

But I see an inconsistency here. The story says that the Egyptians followed the Israelites "into the sea." Why use the word "sea" when earlier the author was using the phrase, "dry land"? Which was it? Dry land or the sea?

The language changes because the character changes. There is not one path through the chaos that we all must tread. God's path for the Egyptians was to let the Israelites go. But Pharaoh

---

[31] There are theories that the Red Sea crossing was possible due to it being a "Sea of Reeds" crossing. While such a concrete explanation is possible, these modernist explanations diminish and in most cases completely ignore the symbolic messages of the story. In this case, the role of chaos and what the author is telling us about the relationship between the chaos, the people, and God is completely ignored by the modernist explanation. (Seiglie, M. See resource #22 in Reference List)

kept saying "No" to that path. In so doing, his kingdom experienced ten plagues (i.e., ten forms of chaos). By pursuing the Israelites, Pharaoh continued to oppose God's offered path through the chaos.

If the Egyptians had listened to God, had let the Israelites go, and stayed in Egypt, then they would have been nowhere *near* the sea to have been swept up by it. But, because they consistently chose to follow their own way, God did not save them from the chaos that their own choices wrought.

Remember, God does not force us to participate in God's better way. We have to choose to participate in the reign of God – that's why Moses' raising of his arm above the sea is an important part of the story. The converse of this also holds true, which is why God does not save (i.e., *force*) Pharaoh from the chaos.

Instead, God just killed Pharaoh and his people!

No. What we see here are the natural consequences of living in and attempting to control the chaos. When we live in the chaos, eventually it destroys us. We saw the same thing in the Noah story: Because the people were not paying attention to God, then they were eventually overwhelmed by the chaos. But with Pharaoh and the Egyptians, God showed patience and compassion for the Egyptians ten separate times.

Patience? *COMPASSION!?* Where do you see God's compassion in this story?

If God did not have compassion and patience for the Egyptians, then God simply would've killed the Egyptians when Pharaoh said "No" the first time. This would've made it much easier for the Israelites, but this is not how God works. God does not force God's will upon us. Furthermore, God knows how scared we are of the chaos and how invested we are in our various systems to try and control it.

Sorry to disappoint you, but *I* am not invested in enslaving other people as a way to keep myself safe from chaos.

It is very difficult for us to let go of the benefits of *mitsrayim* that we believe keep us safe. Just like the Egyptians used the Israelites to buffer themselves against the chaos, so do we, for example, buy food from farms with undocumented and lowly-paid migrant workers, purchase gadgets from tech companies with inhumane working conditions in their supplier factories, and wage wars in other countries (usually in the Middle East) so that we can continue to cheaply power our cars, furnaces, and power plants. So, while you are not literally enslaving people, you *are* invested in and participating in *mitsrayim*.

But before you get defensive, remember that *God has compassion for us,* just like God had compassion for the Egyptians.

Are you *daring* to suggest that my way of life is like the Egyptians?

This is one of the "dangers" of studying the faith stories: We sometimes discover we are not always who we perceive ourselves to be. It is not a journey for the faint of heart. But, even more important than these self-discoveries is the reminder that God never gives up on us; God consistently desires and offers a better way of life for us.

If that's true, then why does it say that God fights the Egyptians in verses 24 through 28?

Because there's definitely some fighting going on. But it is really the Egyptians who are fighting against God and not vice versa. By continually going against the guidance God repeatedly gave them ("Let my people go"), they propelled themselves into the chaos. The longer and harder the Egyptians fought God's direction of how to avoid the chaos, the more they became confused and stuck in the chaos.

So you're saying that the Egyptians received many chances to avoid the chaos, but their stubbornness drove them into the abyss?

Yes, but it was not just stubbornness that drove the Egyptians. One thing to remember about *mitsrayim* is how *attractive* it is to us and how tightly we hold on to it – especially when we benefit from it. To let go of the *mitsrayim* feels like we are inviting death and disaster into our lives, even when it mostly oppresses us (as evidenced by the Israelites' unwillingness to leave Egypt right away).

For another reminder of how potent the temptation of *mitsrayim* is, there's a Gospel story that draws a not-so-subtle comparison between the first-century Israelites and the Egyptians. In the second chapter of Matthew, we're told that King Herod (an Israelite) is worried about a new-born baby (Jesus) who will threaten the current *mitsrayim* – a *mitsrayim* that benefits Herod. So what does Herod do? He orders the killing of all Israelite babies under the age of two.[32] The very thing that Herod's people had experienced and suffered, Herod then inflicts upon his own people (about 1400 years removed from the original event, but *still*)!

---

[32] Matthew 2:16

Ugh! As much as I hate to say, it almost seems like we *can't* escape *mitsrayim*.

Sure we can! But *not* on our own. Just as Moses escaped the killer clutches of *mitsrayim* as a child and then led God's people (with God's help) from oppression to the promised land, Jesus also escaped the *mitsrayim* as a child and then led (with God's help) all of God's children who would listen – including you, us, the poor, the hungry, the tired, and the oppressed – out of the *mitsrayim* and into the reign of God.

Suggested Outline for
CLASS DISCUSSION

1. **Opening Prayer** (1 to 2 minutes)

2. **Opening Question** (10 minutes): *What is something you feel like you don't have enough time to do?*

3. **Read the chapter's scripture passage**

4. **Discussion** (30 to 35 minutes):

   a) Share with the group one or two points in the Context, Scripture Reading, Concepts, and Ruminations sections that you appreciated, disagreed with, struggled to accept or didn't understand.

b) God's path through the chaos for the Egyptians and God's path for the Israelites are pretty different. Is that surprising to you? Why or why not? What do you think are some real-world implications to this understanding that God's way through the chaos isn't necessarily the same for each person?

c) The Israelites had a hard time letting go of their slavery to the Egyptians despite all the serious drawbacks that came with it. Can you think of something in your own life that is oppressive, but you cannot let go of because you think the removal of it would be quite destructive? (Consider this as a way of identifying how the oppression of *mitsrayim* is present in our personal life.)

d) *Follow-up to Question C:* Similar to how the Israelites wanted to return to Egypt after they had been freed, is there something that you have let go of that was of an oppressive nature to you? Did you ever miss it and want to return to it at certain points?

e) Despite intense time constraints (the Egyptians are coming! The Egyptians are coming!), Moses instructs the Israelites to be still. In being still, Moses and the Israelites are able to hear God's instructions about how to navigate their chaotic situation. What are some situations in your everyday life where you think you don't have time to pray?

f) In what ways do you think you experience an advantage due to a practice that is oppressive for other people? (Consider this as a way of identifying how we experience the benefits of *mitsrayim*.)

g) It's possible that, having been alerted to the presence of *mitsrayim* and how it works, you might feel a strong desire to fix it. This is noble, but remember that we cannot control the chaos. When we try to control chaos on our own, we simply displace it. Instead, think of and share ideas with your classmates of how (as an individual and as a group) you can make time to call out to God, be still, listen for God's response, and then act on what you hear.

5. **Discuss details for next class**

6. **Closing Prayer** (3 to 7 minutes)

4. Walking On Water

the DNA of Jesus, prayer
& seven (in)effective habits

□ □ □ ■ □ □

CONTEXT

The last three chapters will center on Jesus and build upon a number of concepts that we've previously identified. We will also discuss how Jesus seeks and follows God's way through the chaos and invites us to do the same.

This chapter's scripture story starts at the end of a difficult day for Jesus. The day began with Jesus receiving news that his cousin (according to the Gospel of Luke) and fellow Good News proclaimer, John the Baptist, was dead – beheaded by King Herod. So Jesus withdrew to a lonely place to pray and grieve. But, a crowd of people followed him. When Jesus saw the crowd, he had compassion for them and healed them. Then, because of the time of day and remote location, food became an issue.

Jesus told his disciples to take care of it, but their solution was to send the people away. This was not acceptable to Jesus. So he took, blessed, and broke five loaves of bread and two fish and gave them to his disciples to share with the crowd. The crowd ate their fill and prepared to return home; it had been a good day for them. But this non-stop, emotionally-taxing day for Jesus was not yet done. Let's see what happened next.

Scripture: *Matthew 14.22-36*

22 Immediately Jesus made the disciples get into the boat and go on ahead to the other side, while he dismissed the crowds. 23 And after he had dismissed the crowds, he went up the mountain by himself to pray. When evening came, he was there alone, 24 but by this time the boat, battered by the waves, was far from the land, for the wind was against them.

25 And early in the morning he came walking toward them on the sea. 26 But when the disciples saw him walking on the sea, they were terrified, saying, "It is a ghost!" And they cried out in fear. 27 But immediately Jesus spoke to them and said, "Take heart, it is I; do not be afraid." 28 Peter answered him, "Lord, if it is you, command me to come to you on the water." 29 He said, "Come."

So Peter got out of the boat, started walking on the water, and came toward Jesus. 30 But when he noticed the strong wind, he became frightened, and beginning to sink, he cried out, "Lord, save me!" 31

Jesus immediately reached out his hand and caught him, saying to him, "You of little faith, why did you doubt?"

32 When they got into the boat, the wind ceased. 33 And those in the boat worshiped him, saying, "Truly you are the Son of God." 34 When they had crossed over, they came to land at Gennesaret. 35 After the people of that place recognized him, they sent word throughout the region and brought all who were sick to him, 36 and begged him that they might touch even the fringe of his cloak; and all who touched it were healed.

CONCEPTS

Disciples - A disciple of a rabbi was less like a student and more like an apprentice. As a disciple, you wanted to do exactly what the rabbi was *doing*. The greatest success a disciple could achieve, then, was to become the rabbi. Jesus expected no less of his own disciples. He even tells them, "I tell you...[you] will also do the works that I do and, in fact, will do greater works than these."[33]

To become like the rabbi, disciples would copy and repeat the practices and actions of one's rabbi. To mimic one's rabbi was a core component of discipleship.[34]

---

[33] John 14:12

Like any apprenticeship, learning what the rabbi taught was a process; mastery was not automatic or guaranteed. Mistakes were made and students would often quit or change rabbis. The best students, however, would not shy from their mistakes, but learn from them and continue forward.

Prayer and God's instruction - Prayer is a conversation with God in which we have two available roles: Talker and listener. Most of us do pretty well with the talking role, but how well do we as listeners?

If we're not listening, it is not because God is a silent God. As we've seen in the last three chapters, God has plenty to say. In Genesis, God speaks creation into being. In the Noah story, we are given insight to God's thoughts and feelings about the current state of affairs (God regretted and was grieved) and then God gives Noah quite the blueprint for quite the boat. Finally, in the parting of the Red Sea story, God instructs Moses to, "Stretch your staff over the sea." In this chapter's story, we do not hear God's words to Jesus. But we do see Jesus' commitment to prayer:

1. Jesus is intentional in creating time and space for prayer.

---

2. Jesus prays for a long period of time and does not let the distraction of the storm interrupt his time of prayer.

Fear - The opposite of trust is fear. Where trust strengthens a relationship, fear will erode it. With Peter, we see how fear, acting in tandem with the chaos, fills and then pulls him into the sea and, at least for the moment, farther away from Jesus.

If we compare Peter's end result with Jesus', then we see that the unafraid one is left standing. This simplification of the story is somewhat unfair to Peter since he was still a student. But Jesus' response to him ("You of little faith") states an expectation of Peter to match Jesus' actions, instead of being afraid and sinking into the chaos.

RUMINATIONS

To be able to best discuss the powerful message and symbolism of Jesus walking on water, we must first start with who Jesus is.

That's easy, because we see at the end of the story that the disciples call him the Son of God.

But what does that mean?

That God is his parent.

But is that unique? For instance, isn't God your parent?

Yes, but not like God is Jesus' parent.

Are you saying that you are less important to God than Jesus is?

No! Well...maybe? Oh, I don't know! What I DO know is that Jesus has divine powers because God is his actual parent.

With that reasoning, how do you explain Peter's ability to walk on water?

Maybe Jesus was able to extend his power to Peter similar to how Superman can fly away with Lois Lane in his arms?

Your analogy of Jesus as Superman implies that later on in the story, Jesus dropped Peter and let him sink.

I think it's more like Peter wiggled himself loose.

Why would Peter do that? He was the one who wanted to walk on the water with Jesus in the first place.

How about this – how about *you* tell *me* what is happening in this story?

As our back-and-forth shows, this can be a difficult story to discuss due to various Christian understandings of Jesus. For instance, there is a significant cross-section of Christianity that would interpret Jesus walking on water just like you did: As proof of Jesus' divinity.

Is there a problem with such an interpretation?

To be blunt, yes. To use this story as proof of Jesus' divinity diminishes Jesus' choices in the story, undermines Jesus' invitation to follow him, and completely ignores the role of chaos in the story. When we (Christians/the Church) reduce Jesus to a supernatural entity, we all lose.

Did you just say identifying Jesus as a supernatural entity *reduces* who he is?

Yes.

That is a very odd thing to say. How exactly does identifying Jesus as a supernatural entity *reduce* him?

Staying free of the chaos is a God-*directed* ability that takes practice. Jesus stays free of the chaos by keeping his attention continually on God. To suggest that Jesus' ability is due to his divine DNA is to render inconsequential the choices Jesus made as a human being. It is not *who* Jesus is that keeps him free of the chaos, but what Jesus *chooses.*

But isn't Jesus, you know, special?

Yes, he is. But again, that is due to the choices he makes and not because of his birth narrative. The implications of this distinction become clear once we apply Jesus' choices to Peter (and ourselves). If Jesus can walk on water because he pays attention to God, then Peter (and the rest of humanity) can do so, too.

Are you saying that if Superman said to the citizens of Metropolis, "Fly like me," and then took off, it would be unfair to expect them to fly after him?

Now you're getting it! If we think Jesus is like Superman, then none of the disciples can *actually* follow Jesus. Instead, they (and the rest of us) can only stand around and wait for "Jesus: The Spiritual Superhero" to rescue us.

Just to be clear – you really are suggesting that the disciples can replicate Jesus' actions?

Not immediately, but yes, that's what it means to be a disciple of Jesus: To learn what Jesus learned. To do what Jesus did. To live like he lived. To practice the spiritual disciplines that he practiced. To focus on God like he focused on God.

How sure are you that it was what Jesus knew and did that kept him above the chaos and not his DNA?

As sure as the Matthew 14:22-36 passage is. The story begins with Jesus making time and space to be still and pray. It is only *after* this time in prayer that Jesus is able to navigate the chaos.

When you say it that way, it sounds like Jesus is doing the same things that the characters did in the other chapters.

That's because he is! In particular, this story closely mirrors Moses' experience of crossing the Red Sea.

How so? At what point does Jesus escape an approaching army intent upon enslaving him?

You're right that Jesus does not escape any armies that are in hot pursuit. But, as we discussed in the previous chapter, the Hebrew word for Egypt, *mitsrayim*, carries with it a strong association of constriction, narrowness, and oppression. Although the factors around Jesus are not exactly the same as the Israelites experienced in the previous chapter's scripture story, Jesus *is* experiencing the stress of *mitsrayim* here.

I don't see that at all. What *mitsrayim* is Jesus experiencing?

Consider the preceding event that led Jesus to originally seek a quiet place: He had just received news that John the Baptist – his friend, ministry partner, and family member (according to Luke) – had been killed by King Herod. If the powers-that-be kill a family member who is also your co-worker, then the odds that you are next are *greatly* increased. While Jesus doesn't have an army breathing down his neck right at that moment, the pressures of *mitsrayim* are steadily encroaching.

To make things worse, a crowd had decided to follow Jesus to the place where he wanted to be alone (thwarting his first attempt to be still). Though not as dangerous as an Egyptian army, a crowd can certainly bring its own pressures, as anyone who has ever engaged in public speaking can attest.

Okay, I can now see how the stress and even threat of violence is similar in both stories.

Another thing that is similar is how the chaos consistently offers reasons to not be still and pray. Remember how unbelievable you thought it was that Moses would instruct the Israelites to be still while the Egyptian army drew near?

Yes, I remember that clearly. It worked out for them, but I STILL say that was some unbelievable advice by Moses.

Then this next part of the story might have the same effect on you: After the crowd leaves, Jesus sends his disciples away and finally has some time to be still and pray. Except – something happens.

You mean the part where the storm appears?

Yes. Although Jesus is not the son of a sailor, there's no doubt that he's aware of the danger that the storm presents to the boat and his disciples. For this reason, it is noteworthy that he does not act right away. The scripture says the storm arrived in the evening, but that Jesus doesn't go to help his disciples until the early morning.[35]

Oh, you're right! Jesus is doing a very similar thing that Moses did – he's being still and praying at a time when he should be acting. But why would Jesus do that to his disciples?

Most likely, Jesus is being still and listening to God so that he'll be able to see the path through the chaos that God can already see.

---

[35] Jesus' plan to pray suffers two interruptions in this story (the crowd and then the storm). This is not a unique experience when planning intentional prayer time – interruptions are common. As we see with Jesus, some flexibility and delay in the face of these interruptions is acceptable, but at the same time, the reasons to delay intentional prayer time will never fully cease. This means, eventually, that one must do like Jesus does and say "No" to the interruptions and make the prayer time the priority.

We can infer that Jesus is hearing from God because of the path Jesus traverses after his prayer time. It should be a familiar path to us by now since it is very similar to the paths that God's spirit, Noah, and Moses also traveled. By being still, Jesus was able to see the dry path that God reveals for him through (or in this case, *above*) the watery chaos.

So why does Jesus have to pray for such a long time before he can walk on water, but Peter is able to walk on water without any prayer at all?

For the same reason that Noah's family floated above the chaos due to Noah's righteousness and all of the Israelites were able to travel through the Red Sea because of Moses' reminder to be still and listen: There is a sphere of influence that surrounds those who prayerfully seek God's path through the chaos.

Because of Jesus' prayerful choices, it is easier for Peter to see God's way. And, that way is attractive to Peter -- he *wants* to travel like Jesus. So he asks to join Jesus above the chaos.

Jesus, who wants his students to learn how to see, know, and walk God's better way, honors Peter's request and invites Peter to give it a try. After all, this is the reason for Jesus' ministry: To show and teach others how to experience the reign of God in the here and now.

Got it! But why, then, is it so easy to go off the path and into the chaos? Peter is able to stay free of the chaos for, what? Maybe two minutes?! Why did God make the dry path so narrow and difficult to stay on?

An apt phrase from driver's training comes to mind: *You go where you're looking, so look where you're going!* Your question of God's path being so narrow puts the blame on God. But that's not the problem. It is a lack of focus that is to blame.

You're blaming Peter's lack of focus as the reason for his sinking?

Partially, yes.

No one shifted Peter's attention for him. He did that all on his own and that shift in attention was crucial. The story tells us that Peter "noticed the strong wind," "became frightened," and then, and only then, began to sink. This is simple cause and effect. Action A plus action B lead to action C.

When Peter is looking to Jesus, he is able to do exactly what Jesus is doing. Once Peter changes his focus from Jesus to the strength of the storm, then his direction also changes and he descends into the sea.

But big waves are scary – I would look at them, too!

Which means you can empathize with Peter's struggles with discipleship: Paying attention to God and following God's better way through the chaos *is* a difficult skill set to learn.

But, Peter is not just learning new skills. He is also *unlearning* a lifetime of societal and cultural teachings (born of *mitsrayim*) that have incorrectly taught him to *survive, manage,* and *overcome* the chaos.

You've been clear in these past few chapters that we can't overcome or manage the chaos. But why would we not want to survive the chaos?

This is a counter-intuitive point: The more we strive to survive the chaos (by managing it or fighting it), the more mired in the chaos we become.[36] For instance, from Chapter 1, we see Marduk from the *Enuma Elish* "defeat" the chaos (i.e., *Tiamat*), which is a form of survival, right? But Marduk is never actually free of the chaos. In fact, directly after the fight, he actually spreads the *Tiamat* all around him. He's more immersed in it than ever at that point!

---

[36] This *could* be interpreted as "So if I just ignore the chaos, my problems will go away." But that is not the message being offered here. Problems / chaos do *not* just go away. The storm doesn't go away until *after* Jesus prays and then *acts* upon what he hears in prayer. The Red Sea does not part until *after* Moses prays and then *lifts* his staff across the sea. The point, here, is to seek God's guidance regarding how to respond to the chaos and to then act accordingly – which is a far different approach than simply ignoring the chaos.

But there has to be a reason for why we think we can survive, manage, and overcome the chaos, right?

Yes, there is a reason: To a limited and temporary extent, our attempts to survive, manage, and overcome the chaos *work*. Marduk thought he had won. Egypt thought that they were on top of the world. *Mitsrayim* doesn't work perfectly, and never forever, but in the short-term, it *can* be moderately successful.

For a more modern example, think of the book, *The Seven Habits of Highly Effective People.* It was a bestseller because those seven habits help organize and navigate the chaos better than other habits do. Thus, we teach these rules to one another. Unfortunately, in so doing, we reinforce the notion that we can manage the chaos on our own.

I think you're just jealous of the book's success!

Not jealous, but concerned. There's this phrase, "Know your friends well, but know your enemy better." *Seven Habits* and similar self-help books encourage us to better know our enemy (chaos) with the promise that we'll then be able to conquer it.

But to know the chaos better, we have to study it. And the more we study it, the more committed we are to making the same mistake that Peter makes in this chapter's scripture story: We turn our attention towards the chaos and then sink into it.

So, in summary, focus on God and not on the habits that we think will help us survive, manage, and then overcome the chaos?

Exactly!

This seems important. Why haven't I learned about this in Sunday school, Bible study, or worship services?

Although the Church is *supposed to* help us focus on God, it has mostly devolved into a religious version of the *Seven Habits* book, where it focuses on the right actions and beliefs we are supposed to have, instead of focusing on God.

Wait – did you just say that the Church doesn't help us focus on God?!?

Yes. From the pulpit, from TV evangelists, from Christian radio, from books about Christianity, etc., we are inundated with instructions to do the right actions and believe the right beliefs.

Hang on – *are you out of your mind*? Right actions and right beliefs *are* what save us! Following those rules is *how* we pay attention to God!

No, that is not true. *Rules and beliefs do not save us from the chaos.* The only way Noah, Moses, and Jesus become aware of God's path through the chaos is through *prayer,* more specifically, *listening prayer.*

Furthermore, paying attention to the right rules and beliefs is not the same thing as paying attention to God. Rules and beliefs will *not* show us the way through the chaos. Simply believing in Jesus Christ as our Lord and Savior will *not* keep us above the chaos. Giving money to the poor will *not* lead us to dry land. And most certainly, attending church committee meetings will *not* encourage us to keep our focus on God.

As the Church, as the Body of Christ, we are meant to remind and encourage each other on a daily basis to keep our eyes on Jesus and listen to God in prayer so that we can know God's way through and above the chaos.

But instead, the Church's narrow focus on "right beliefs" and "right actions" actually encourages the shifting of one's attention *away* from God, which, as we see with Peter, only results in sinking us deeper into the chaos.

Don't you think this is a bit too extreme? I mean, you're arguing against pretty much all of Christianity!

But this isn't an *argument*. It is a call to return our focus to God. For instance, when Jesus asks Peter, "You of little faith, why did you doubt," is Jesus arguing with Peter? Is he being too extreme? Or is Jesus helping Peter think about why he deviated from God's dry path? And wouldn't this same question apply to any person or institution that finds itself mired in the chaos?

Far be it from me to argue with Jesus...but, maybe, just maybe, Jesus *is* expecting too much?

No, he's not. Jesus is providing Peter an analytical tool to determine why he stopped paying attention to Jesus and started paying attention to the chaos. How is that too great of an expectation? And if we choose to follow Jesus, then the same question needs to be applied to us: Why do we veer off God's dry path and into the chaos?

I think I know your answer to that question! We veer off into the chaos because we pay attention to it and try to manage it.

YES!

But this answer assumes that it is actually possible to avoid veering into the chaos.

That's because it IS possible to not veer into the chaos! This is what Jesus models throughout his ministry and calls us to replicate!

However, if we think of "Jesus as Superman" then we cannot fathom this possibility. If we think of Jesus as Superman, then our own responsibility is reduced to believing (and possibly telling others) that Jesus will save us, just like Superman saves Lois Lane.

Just to be clear, you are saying that the story says that we *can* do what Jesus did, right?

Yes! But (and this is important), it depends on how badly we want it. It takes work and dedication to do like Jesus did. As we see with Peter in this chapter's story, he can do what Jesus did, just not as well – because doing what Jesus does is *not* an instantaneous metamorphosis. There *will* be sinking setbacks.

And, to be fair to Peter and the rest of us, this is what it means to be an apprentice. It is a process and in that process, we will make mistakes. But if we persevere, if we continue to choose to follow and be a disciple of Jesus, then our entire approach to life will be transformed.

Our entire approach to life will be *transformed*?

It sounds big because it is; this is why Jesus refers to it as being "born again" (or "born from above").[37] This is also why Jesus says, "Those who lose their life will keep it."[38] To follow Jesus one hundred percent, to do what Jesus does, is to let go of the world's way of surviving the chaos ("focusing on human things") and to instead embrace God's better way of living ("focusing on the divine").

This is a daunting list that you're making here: Hard work. Tough choices. Saying no to conventional wisdom. High expectations. Sinking setbacks. Why even try?

When we choose to be "born from above," we are then living as vessels of God's hope, life, and light to those overwhelmed by the chaos – just like Jesus pulled Peter immediately from the sea, just like Moses led the Israelites out of the *mitsrayim*, and just like Noah's ark carried a diverse and abundant array of life above the chaos. It's the better way for us and it's the better way for those who are near us.

That *does* sound good, but some of the things you are saying are so different than what most everyone else is saying – it's hard to know who is right.

---

[37] John 3:3
[38] Luke 17:33

Yes, *mitsrayim* and the belief that we can manage the chaos is a widely-accepted practice that infiltrates every dimension of our society, including religion. But this is not a way of life or approach that Jesus subscribes to – which is why the next two chapters will include aspects of how Jesus disrupts and challenges the status quo in society and his religion by living in God's reign.

Suggested Outline for
CLASS DISCUSSION

1. **Opening Prayer** (1 to 2 minutes)

2. **Opening Question** (10 minutes): *What is something that you practice (or used to practice) on a regular basis?*

3. **Read the chapter's scripture passage out loud**

4. **Discussion** (30 to 35 minutes):

    a) Share with the group one or two points in the Context, Scripture Reading, Concepts, and Ruminations sections that you appreciated, disagreed with, struggled to accept or didn't understand.

b) After a long and difficult day, Jesus chooses to end it in solitude and prayer. When a day is long and difficult for you, how do you usually end it?

c) First, Jesus goes to a deserted place to be alone and a crowd follows him. Then, he sends his disciples away, and a storm appears and endangers the disciples. It's almost like there's an active force trying to keep Jesus from praying. What events and distractions keep you from praying?

d) Near the end of the scripture story, Jesus is a little bit annoyed with Peter for sinking which suggests that he expects Peter to be able to do exactly what he, Jesus, does. What do you think it means to follow Jesus and what do you think should be the result of following him?

e) One of the interesting things about Peter's sinking is that he doesn't drop like a rock to the bottom of the sea. Instead of sinking all the way to the bottom, he is instead mired in the chaos. Jesus then pulls him out. In what way(s) do you feel Jesus helps you (or could help you) get unstuck from the chaos?

f) Peter sinks into the chaos because he's been trained to pay attention to it by surviving, managing, and overcoming it. What are some of your own time-honored, battle-tested *7 highly effective strategies* to survive, manage, and overcome the chaos?

g) *Follow-up to Question F:* What *7 highly effective strategies* do you think your church employs to navigate the chaos, and thereby teaches to the congregation as well?

5. **Discuss details for next class**

6. **Closing Prayer** (3 to 7 minutes)

5. Jesus & the Gerasene Man

unclean spirits, a reverse flood & salvation

□　□　□　◘　■　□

CONTEXT

The story of the Gerasene demoniac is told in Matthew, Mark, and Luke. In each telling, the story is nestled in a sequence of events that serves to cement Jesus' identity as Messiah (the anointed one). In the Gospel of Mark, for example, Jesus calms the storm, steps out of the boat in the land of the Gerasenes to cast out a fearsome demoniac (that's this chapter's story), then returns to his homeland where he raises a girl from the dead.

The land of the Gerasenes and its surrounding neighbors (sometimes referred to as the "Decapolis") shared a recent and violent history with the Israelites leading up to Jesus' lifetime. The increasing influence of Hellenism (i.e., Greek culture and civilization that was introduced when Alexander the Great conquered the area) led to growing unease in and around Jerusalem that eventually culminated in the successful rebellion of the Maccabees. This rebellion freed Jerusalem from the

106

Seleucid Empire in 164 B.C.E. In the following years, the Israelites strengthened and extended their borders. Israelite control over the Decapolis region was mostly contentious during this time. Then, in 64 B.C.E., Pompey and the Romans arrived and defeated everyone, ending military conflicts between neighboring areas.[39]

One result of these cultural and military conflicts was the rise of the Pharisees and their influence. Their fanaticism for Torah was a rule-based reaction to Hellenistic humanism (best summarized as "a celebration of humanity") that was attractive to some of the Israelites. The Pharisees viewed humanism as idolatry, as a form of worship of humankind. By promoting and demanding strict adherence to their traditional rules (a.k.a., Mosaic Law), the Pharisees continued to resist Hellenism, even with the Romans in charge.[40]

For all of these reasons, then, Jesus' visit to the Decapolis would have been immediately understood by a first-century Israelite as a dangerous foray into enemy culture and territory.

---

[39] A Far Country—Decapolis. See resource #1 in Reference List
[40] Hellenism: Center of the Universe See resource #14 in Reference List

Scripture: Mark 5:1-20

1 *Jesus and his disciples came to the other side of the sea, to the country of the Gerasenes. 2 And when he had stepped out of the boat, immediately a man out of the tombs with an* **unclean spirit** *met him. 3 He lived among the tombs; and no one could restrain him any more, even with a chain; 4 for he had often been restrained with shackles and chains, but the chains he wrenched apart, and the shackles he broke in pieces; and no one had the strength to subdue him. 5 Night and day among the tombs and on the mountains he was always howling and bruising himself with stones. 6 When he saw Jesus from a distance, he ran and bowed down before him; 7 and he shouted at the top of his voice, "What have you to do with me, Jesus, Son of the Most High God? I adjure you by God, do not torment me." 8 For Jesus had said to him, "Come out of the man, you unclean spirit!"*

9 Then Jesus asked him, "What is your name?" He replied, "My name is **Legion***; for we are many." 10 He begged him earnestly not to send them out of the country. 11 Now there on the hillside a great herd of swine was feeding; 12 and the unclean spirits begged him, "Send us into the* **swine***; let us enter them." 13 So Jesus gave them permission. And the unclean spirits came out and entered the swine; and the herd, numbering about two thousand, rushed down the steep bank into the sea, and were drowned in the sea. 14 The swineherds ran off and told it in the city and in the country. Then people came to see what it was that had happened.*

15 They came to Jesus and saw the demoniac sitting there, clothed and in his right mind, the very man who had had the legion; and they were afraid. 16 Those who had seen what had happened to the demoniac and to the swine reported it. 17 Then they began to beg Jesus to leave their neighborhood. 18 As he was getting into the boat, the man who had been possessed by demons begged him that he might be with him. 19 But Jesus refused, and said to him, "Go home to your friends, and tell them how much the Lord has done for you, and what mercy he has shown you." 20 And he went away and began to proclaim in the Decapolis how much Jesus had done for him; and everyone was amazed.

CONCEPTS

Unclean Spirits - The Greek word for "unclean" also translates as "dirty" or "polluted." The Greek word for "spirit" is *pneuma* (which is where *pneumonia* derives from, for instance). *Pneuma*, like its Hebrew counterpart, *ruach*, can mean wind, breath and/or spirit. The phrase "unclean spirit," then, could just as easily be translated as "dirty wind" or "polluted air" or "foul breath." The different possible translations are important to keep in mind because otherwise it is too easy to read "unclean spirit" as a condition of being possessed by a supernatural force.

The actual phrase of "unclean spirit" is used rather generically in the scripture stories and is applied to a number of afflictions (psychological and physiological) to which, today, we would apply specific names, such as "schizophrenia," "epilepsy," and "the flu."

Current practices treat these afflictions with medication and coping strategies. But the Biblical stories offer another response: Cast it out.

This casting out is usually a dramatic event in the Bible stories. The person with the unclean spirit often thrashes about and screams to the point of appearing dead at the end of their spiritual tantrum.[41]

Legion - Legion was the term for the largest and most basic Roman army unit, consisting of 5,000 soldiers. To use this name for one's unclean spirit is most likely meant to draw comparisons to the fearsome power of Rome's military strength and its accompanying oppressive, occupying power.

Swine - Spirits were not the only things Israelites considered unclean. They also had strict dietary rules that called certain foods "clean" (okay to eat) and other foods "unclean" (not okay to eat). Pigs, for example, were in the "unclean" food category. The large number of pigs in this chapter's story tells us

---

[41] For example, Mark 9:26

that the pigs were an important part of the town's diet *and* economy. Since a large part of the town's diet and economy were based on unclean food, it would have been no surprise to a first-century Israelite that this town also had outsized unclean spirits.

RUMINATIONS

Promise me that you will talk about the pigs – I have so many questions about the pigs! Why did the pigs run into the sea? Did Jesus know the pigs were going to run into the sea? Why does Jesus let the unclean spirit of "Legion" go into the pigs in the first place? *Why is this story so weird!?*

It *is* a strange story, and yes, we'll talk about the pigs. As we identify some of the symbolism, the story will hopefully start to make more sense. Sorting through the symbolism, though, will keep us from immediately addressing all of your pig questions.

That's alright, just don't forget! As for symbols in the story, I already know that the sea can be a symbol of chaos. But the sea doesn't seem very important in this story, it just *sits* there.

You're right, the sea *does* just sit there. But, the problem is that not *all* of the chaos is sitting there. To repeat a footnote from

Chapter 1, chaos is like dirty laundry. It is not good or bad, but it does need to be correctly stored. It is meant to be stored in the hamper (the sea) and not on the floor (dry land).

So where is the chaos being incorrectly stored in this story?

In the pigs.

I thought so! But how can you be sure?

Once the unclean pigs and the unclean spirit join forces, we see that they then "merge" with the sea. Pair that end result with our newly-gleaned understandings from chapter 2 about the relationship between chaos and creation and the conclusion appears to be quite clear: The pigs are a symbol of incorrectly stored chaos.

What specific information have I gleaned from chapter 2?

That too much chaos in one place undoes the definition of creation. The chaos of the unclean spirit plus the incorrectly stored chaos of the pigs is just too much chaos and leads to creation (the herd of pigs) coming undone.

Ah, I think I get it – it's like the addition of the unclean spirit is the final straw of chaos that broke the pigs' back!

That's a good way to think of it.

But why would Jesus agree to send the unclean spirit into the herd of pigs?

Common sense. To a first-century Israelite, the placing of unclean spirits into pigs that then run into the sea is no different than a twenty-first-century American throwing trash into a dumpster that is then emptied into a landfill. Jesus is simply cleaning up. He is helping to undo the undoing of creation.

What do you mean by "undo the undoing of creation?"

In the Noah chapter, we saw how the people participated in the undoing of creation. In this chapter, we see how Jesus *reverses* that undoing of creation. The Noah story showed how chaos was invited onto the dry land where it did not belong. This story illustrates how Jesus returns the chaos to where it *does* belong. In other words, this is an *anti*-flood story.

So Jesus is participating in a symbolic land reclamation project?

More specifically, Jesus is participating in a reclamation of *us*. This is how Jesus saves *us*.

Where did that come from? Why are you talking about Jesus saving us when there has been no mention of heaven or hell?

Because salvation is not *primarily* about where we go after we die.

The salvation that I know is where Jesus saves me from my sins. If I believe in Jesus, then I get to live with God in heaven after I die. What other salvation could there possibly be?

For starters, there is the salvation that the Gerasene man receives: Salvation from internalized chaos. Subsequently, the man is also saved from the attempts the townspeople made at controlling his internalized chaos (a.k.a. the *mitsrayim*).

Okay, so far that doesn't seem to be an argument against salvation as I understand it...

Because it isn't. But it is an encouragement to understand "salvation" in a broader context. For instance, "eternal life" is usually understood to refer to life *after* death. But eternal life can begin *now* (if only for the reason that there is no start or end to eternity). This is good news for the Gerasene man because it means that he can experience God's eternal life while he is alive instead of having to wait until he dies.

That makes sense, but in general I think most of us tend to think about salvation in terms of where we go when we die, and not so much from certain ways of living.

To the detriment of us all! But, thankfully, this is not how Jesus understood salvation. So let's talk some about the actual encounter between Jesus and the Gerasene man since it illustrates one way we can be saved in the here and now.

Okay, but only if you go slowly. It feels like we've been going 100 miles per hour so far!

How the story describes the Gerasene man helps set the stage. He did not live in any way that we would consider normal. He lived in a cemetery (where the bodies would have been decaying in the caves – not pleasant!). He howled day and night. He hit himself with rocks.

It's like he's the Incredible Hulk of chaos.

Yes! He is an embodiment of chaos. So, what did the town do to help him with his situation?

I don't know if it was an attempt to help *him*, but the story says they bound him with chains and shackles.

Which proved unsuccessful. They also ostracized him – he was not allowed to live in the town with them.

Maybe they were not the most competent of townspeople? Or maybe they just weren't very caring people?

Or, maybe, like we discussed in chapters 3 and 4, the townspeople were simply trying their best to survive, manage, and control the chaos. They were applying their 7 (in)effective habits to organize and navigate the chaos, but the result was the same outcome we've seen in all the other stories: They could not win the fight against the chaos nor could they overcome it. The result, then, was that both the man and the town were oppressed by the man's chaotic state.

But isn't that because he's *very* chaotic? I find this guy impossible to relate to – I do NOT have these problems!

It is true that the level of the Gerasene man's internal chaos is extreme, which serves two purposes for us. One, it allows us to all agree that the man is not alright – *something* is wrong with him. Two, his ensuing salvation illustrates that the same option is available to us. Regardless of how powerful, scary, or crazy our chaotic circumstances may appear, they are not scarier, crazier, or more powerful than the Gerasene demoniac. If God's salvation is available to this man and "works" for him, then God's salvation is available to us and will "work" for us, too.

However, we may not know how to access this salvation. The townspeople certainly did not, nor did the Gerasene man –

which is why it was a good thing that Jesus, the embodiment of God's defining Word, arrives.

The first time I read this, I thought there might be a physical conflict when the Gerasene man approached Jesus. I was expecting a classic showdown between good and evil!

Yes, conflict appears to be unavoidable. Enculturated as we are by Hollywood special effects, an action scene seems most appropriate here. Imagine a ninja-styled sword fight between the Gerasene man and Jesus while the disciples and some werewolves(!) fire laser guns at each other, in the middle of the night, with flashes of lightning brightening the cloudy sky! Pretty cool, right? Because this is where Jesus the Good conquers Legion the Bad.

Yes! Awesome! Where have you been this whole book!? You've finally found your writing style!

Except, sorry, that's not how the story goes.

Oh yeah. Right.

There is not one peal of thunder, not one thrown punch, not even an Elvis-like lip snarl. Because, remember, this is not a battle for supremacy between two equal but separate powers of

Good and Evil. Instead, this is a human being who is filled with chaos and is seeking exodus from his internal condition.

How do you know the Gerasene man desires an "exodus from his internal condition?"

Because, when he reaches Jesus, he *bows down* to Jesus. His bowing gives us a glimpse of his inner-self that longs for everlasting life. Still alive in the Gerasene man is someone who wants to live as he was made to live. This person is difficult to see, though, because of the tantrum that follows Jesus' initial and failed attempt at casting out the man's unclean spirit.

Jesus fails?

Failure is probably too strong of a word, but yes, Jesus' first attempt is not successful (*vv.* 7-8).[42] The demoniac is not obedient or complacent to Jesus' command, but instead screams at Jesus, "Why do you torment me?"

Wait a minute! You just said that the Gerasene man wanted help and that that's why he bowed to Jesus blah blah blah. But now you're saying the Gerasene man is *resisting* Jesus. Which is it!?

---

[42] The other two "unsuccessful" Jesus healing stories: When healing a blind man, upon the first try, the blind man can only see "trees walking around" (Mark 8:22-26). And then, when visiting his hometown, Jesus is amazed at how few people he can heal due to their lack of faith (Mark 6:5-6).

It turns out that there *is* a battle in this story, but that battle takes place *inside* the Gerasene man. The struggle is not between the man and Jesus, but between the man's internalized voice of chaos (Legion) and the voice inside the man that says "There's got to be a better way – I just know it!"

The voice of Legion seems similar to the voice of the Israelites that kept telling Moses to leave them with the Egyptians.

Yes! Our attachment to the things that oppress us is universal.

You know, I don't mean to be silly, but I'm having an irreverent thought about these internal voices.

Please share!

Occasionally, I will overeat. Afterwards, I might even say something, like, "Dinner was great, but I'm so stuffed that I can barely breathe." But then, there's this little voice in my head that says, "*Don't forget about dessert.*"

Then what happens?

I usually have dessert...

Yes, that's perfect! Even when they make no sense, our internal voices can be incredibly compelling. Your "silly" example helps us to consider why the Gerasene man would still listen to the voice of "Legion" even as he seeks to be free of it.

Is this why Jesus is undeterred by the man's outburst of defiance?

Most likely, but also notice that Jesus *does* change tactics. After his first attempt, Jesus then asks the man what his name is. The man replies with a name to the voice he was just listening to, "Legion."

Is the actual name, "Legion," significant?

It certainly is striking that the man uses the largest, most common fighting force in his known world to describe his internal condition. The usage of the word would also strike a chord with a first-century Israelite, since the Roman legion had been instrumental in the defeat of Israel.

With this in mind, we see how Jesus' overall response to the man is just as significant as the name the Gerasene man offers. At no point does Jesus fight or argue with this oppressive, occupying legion, similar to how Moses and the Israelites did not fight against the Egyptians and how God did not fight the chaos in the creation story.

Instead, Jesus offers the man God's salvation from the oppressive force. We see that salvation take hold once the man utters the name of what oppresses him.

Where do you see salvation being offered and *how* is it being offered? I don't see it.

Until this moment, the details of the story have focused on the man's imposing presence, his sheer physicality and force. Even Jesus can't stop him! But once the man is provided an opportunity to name the voice that drives him, once that internalized chaos is named, then the power of God's Word (re)asserts itself upon the chaos.

This is the turning point in the story. Once the man gives a name to the chaos, then it is defined. And defined chaos is, by definition, no longer chaos. Which is why, once "Legion" is named, the focus of the story shifts from the man's imposing presence to other details such as where "Legion" will go, what the pigs do, and how the townspeople respond.

I think I'm starting to understand...You know, once you start to put everything together from the previous chapters (the power of words, how we corrupt the land by inviting chaos in, *mitsrayim*, etc.) I'm realizing how amazingly brilliant this story is. I am in awe, really, of how it all fits together!

It is, indeed, some impressive storytelling.

But, here's another question – if the chaos was transformed, then why does it need to still leave the man and go into the pigs?

Once the chaos is defined, then it is separate from the man. The man is restored to his right mind because the chaos is no longer embedded into his being. But, the chaos is still *in* him. For example, think about when you cough up phlegm. There's a few moments, there, where the phlegm is separate from your lungs, but it is still in your body (more specifically, in your mouth).

Yuck!

Sorry about the visual, but it is as helpful as it is disgusting. Once the phlegm is separated from the lungs, it still needs to be put elsewhere, preferably outside of the body. This is why the man and Jesus discuss where this separated piece of chaos should be placed. They agree on the pigs.

Can you explain why Jesus and the man choose the pigs? Why not just send the unclean spirit straight into the sea at this point?

We don't know for sure because there is no given explanation. But, one way to think about this part of the story is to think about how salvation from the chaos works.

What do you mean?

When we accept and participate in our salvation to live free of the chaos, then, with God's help, we are reversing the flow of the chaos. And when you reverse the flow of something, that something must be returned to where it originated.

So for the man to really experience salvation, the chaos that the Gerasenes had invited into their community in the form of pigs also had to be addressed?

That's certainly one way to interpret this part of the story. When you look at it this way, you also start to see how radical and expensive such salvation from the chaos and *mitsrayim* can be. In this case, it cost the town two thousand pigs, which would have had an immediate and direct effect on the Gerasenes' diet and bank accounts. Even if the number is an overstatement, the idea being conveyed is that freedom from the chaos and *mitsrayim* results in a major restructuring of society. For the Egyptians, losing a cheap labor force was a big deal. In this case, the economic structure of the Gerasenes was gutted.

No wonder the townspeople told Jesus to leave!

Remarkably, the cost of the man's salvation was not what disturbed the townspeople the most. The story tells us that the townspeople were most troubled by seeing the Gerasene demoniac in his right mind and in regular clothes (*vv.* 15).

Why would a man being restored to his right mind frighten the townspeople?

The town's "normal" life had included a crazy man. But suddenly there was a *new* normal in town and it had emerged without their permission. In other words, a power greater than their seven (in)effective habits was on full display.

So what? Why is that a problem?

When we are not the ones controlling the deployment of said greater power, then we suddenly realize that our control of the situation was not as great as we initially thought. This realization (that we lack the power we thought we had) will *always* scare us. In this case, the townspeople were so frightened that they told Jesus to leave.

This is a different pushing away of Jesus than occurred earlier in the story when the Legion man was conflicted, right? He wanted Jesus' help and tried to push Jesus away at the same time.

Right. We know that the townspeople do *not* desire salvation from their way of life because they do not bow down to Jesus. It is also telling that Jesus agrees to leave.

The more we discuss this story, the more I marvel at it! But the militaristic tones that are not acted upon leave me surprised that there wasn't at least a *little* violence.

The belief that violence is needed to fix what is broken in the world *is* a long-held one.

Because "might makes right," right?

That's how the saying goes and the Israelites were not immune to holding similar beliefs. For instance, many first-century Israelites believed that the Messiah would, through militaristic means, free Israel from political oppression and outsider influence. The Messiah was also expected to expand the political might of the Israelite people, far greater than even King David did. Jesus, in this light, was quite the disappointment. He did not overcome the current *mitsrayim* regime (Rome), nor create a Jewish empire in its place.

Doesn't this story refute a number of those disappointments, though?

How so?

Jesus just "defeated" a Roman legion. And, he teaches anyone who chooses to follow him how to access and live in a better kingdom: the reign of God / the kingdom of God.

Good points! And, it is within this context that it is best to consider the militaristic language that does appear in scripture (e.g., when Paul talks about putting on the armor of God and the shield of faith).[43] This language does have its place, especially if we understand the internal spiritual battle that we face. But, the language often gets misconstrued with our national, militaristic cultures, which brings a story to mind–

Well, don't hold back! Do tell!

Ray, a church member, was conversing with his pastor about why "Onward Christian Soldiers" was left out of a new hymnal. After an explanation from the pastor about avoiding militaristic imagery that could be misconstrued as supporting war and conflict with other religions, Ray responded.

"I understand better than many people the horror of war, because I saw it first-hand in Korea. And I wonder if the people that put together the new hymnals think we're all idiots. I know that hymn is not about taking up arms against Muslims or Catholics or pagans. I know that the song is not encouraging us to drop bombs on our so-called enemies. I also know that when I sing it, I am reminded that the choice to be faithful – to live like Jesus – is an everyday battle. I am reminded that the cross of Jesus goes before me and that the battle is hard. But by God's power, the battle is already won."

---

[43] Ephesians 6:13-18

Oh, that's good. Amen, Brother Ray! Amen!

As Ray says, the real battle is the choice to live like Jesus, to receive the salvation that Jesus offers as the embodiment of God's unfettered word. The battle, though, is an internal one instead of a physical one. It is a battle where we fight to consistently request and constantly welcome God's word into our internal lives.

When we make this choice to follow God's direction and walk free of the chaos, then we are reversing the outward flow of chaos. With God's help, we undo the flood of chaos by being God's gift and blessing in a chaotic world. Our salvation transforms us into islands of dry land that can then be experiences of respite to our swamped neighbors.

This is no easy task, and don't expect the beneficiaries of *mitsrayim* to welcome your salvation from the chaos. Instead, expect the same treatment that Jesus received from the townspeople – they will ask you, in various forms, to leave or revert to your previous ways of living. This temptation and pressure to revert to the ways of old will be very strong. This is why, in the next chapter, we'll look at how Jesus invites and teaches us how to *keep* living in the reign of God.

Suggested Outline for
CLASS DISCUSSION

1. **Opening Prayer** (1 to 2 minutes)

2. **Opening Question** (10 minutes): *What is an unhealthy or unlikeable habit of yours that you cannot seem to break?*

3. **Read the chapter's scripture passage**

4. **Discussion** (30 to 35 minutes):

   a) Share with the group one or two points in the Context, Scripture Reading, Concepts, and Ruminations sections that you appreciated, disagreed with, struggled to accept or didn't understand.

   b) As a way to think about the internal conflict that the Gerasene man seemed to experience when talking to Jesus, there was a "silly" example in the *Ruminations* section of an internal voice that would advocate for dessert after a very filling dinner. Have you ever had similar internal arguments (silly or otherwise)? If yes, what is an example of an internal argument that you have had with yourself?

   c) As noted in the Ruminations section, the naming of the unclean spirit(s) is what marks the turning point in the story for Jesus and the Gerasene man. What descriptive names might you give to the internal voices that argue/compete for your attention?

d) The concept of salvation was broadly defined in the *Ruminations* section, mentioning that God's everlasting life for us can begin now, not just after we die. We then saw in the story how the Gerasene man received salvation from his internal chaos. What internal chaos do you regularly experience that you might ask God to save you from?

e) What do you think about the idea that your personal salvation from a chaos-filled life serves as the beginning of your community's salvation from a chaos-filled life?

f) In many ways, this is the climatic chapter of the book. Most, if not all, of the symbolism and concepts that you learned in the previous chapters were put to use in deciphering and understanding the Gerasene demoniac story: The symbolism of the sea and dry land, the power of language, the undoing of creation, the effect(s) of *mitsrayim*, 7 (in)effective habits, etc. Do you find yourself applying these concepts to other stories (Biblical or otherwise) as well? Maybe even to situations in your own life? And, are there any concepts that stick in your mind more than others as you move through your day/week?

5. **Discuss details for next class**

6. **Closing Prayer** (3 to 7 minutes)

6. Jesus Calls Disciples

breaking tradition, a fish out of water
& leaving everything behind

❒ ❑ ❑ ❑ ❑ ■

CONTEXT

We do not have much information about how Jesus became a rabbi. What we do know is that Jesus showed promise at the age of twelve when he amazed the Temple scribes with his questions and insights (Luke 2:41-47). We also know that he could read (Luke 4:16-21), an ability available to a select few (possibly only 3% of the population) and a needed skill for rabbis.[44] Finally, we know that the people around him, including those who were not his disciples, called him "Rabbi" (usually translated as "Teacher" in English).

Typically, to become a rabbi, a young man would choose to become a disciple (or "student") of another rabbi. The traditional approach of "enrollment" was for the young man to ask a rabbi permission to become his disciple. Usually, it was only the

---

[44] Bar-Ilan, M. See resource #3 in Reference List
Evans, C. See resource #12 in Reference List

smartest and brightest disciples who were able to proceed far enough to then become a rabbi in their own right.[45]

With this cultural context in mind, we can better understand Jesus' break from tradition when he calls his own disciples. By selecting various types of people (fishermen, women, tax collectors, zealots, etc.) to be his disciples, Jesus signaled a different message than the elite rabbinical system. Instead of excluding folks from his position, Jesus invited people from all walks of life to achieve his position.[46]

In this chapter's scripture passage, we will see a number of bold messages in Jesus' invitation to Peter, James, and John to be his disciples.

1. He asks individuals to follow him (instead of waiting for students to approach him).

2. He invites people who were in other lines of work and not dedicated to becoming a rabbi.

3. And, because these individuals were not dedicated disciples in the traditional sense, we see that the usual elite preparation for being a disciple did not concern Jesus. What *was* required to be a disciple of Jesus, though, was an affirmative answer to his invitation.

---

[45] Rabbi and Talmidim... See resource #20 in Reference List
[46] Kogler, K. See resource #19 in Reference List

Scripture: Luke 5:1-11

*1 Once while Jesus was standing beside the **lake of Gennesaret**, and the crowd was pressing in on him to hear the word of God, 2 he saw two boats there at the **shore of the lake**; the fishermen had gone out of them and were washing their nets. 3 He got into one of the boats, the one belonging to **Simon**, and asked him to put out a little way from the shore. Then he sat down and taught the crowds from the boat. 4 When he had finished speaking, he said to Simon, "Put out into the deep water and let down your nets for a catch." 5 Simon answered, "Master, we have worked all night long but have caught nothing. Yet if you say so, I will let down the nets." 6 When they had done this, they caught so many fish that their nets were beginning to break. 7 So they signaled their partners in the other boat to come and help them. And they came and filled both boats, so that they began to sink. 8 But when Simon Peter saw it, he fell down at Jesus' knees, saying, "Go away from me, Lord, for I am a **sinful** man!" 9 For he and all who were with him were amazed at the catch of fish that they had taken; 10 and so also were James and John, sons of Zebedee, who were partners with Simon. Then Jesus said to Simon, "Do not be afraid; from now on you will be catching people." 11 When they had brought their boats to shore, they left everything and followed him.*

CONCEPTS

Lake of Gennesaret is one of the many names for the Sea of Galilee.

The shoreline – Three of the six stories we've read (crossing the Red sea, the Gerasene man, and the calling of Peter, James, and John) take place on the shore, that thin line where water and land overlap. It is a place of transition for biological life in terms of birth cycles, metamorphosis, and evolutionary adaptations that are prompted by the engagement of a new and different living environment. In the faith stories, the shore serves as a symbol for a similar type of transition – a theological transition. It is often the place where characters in the stories consider leaving the chaos to live in the reign of God (and then do so).

Simon means "[God] has heard." Jesus later changes Simon's name to Peter (which means "rock") when telling him, "I will build my church upon you."[47] Because Peter is portrayed as an enthusiastic, but mostly inept student in the Gospel stories, his transformation in the book of Acts to "leader" and "apostle" is nothing short of astonishing. In the Gospels, we see an impetuous, head-strong, slow-learning student. In Acts, we see a changed man; a leader filled with God's Holy Spirit, who heals

---

[47] Matthew 16:17-18

the sick and speaks with authority. Jesus' approach to calling disciples was unorthodox, but it was also effective.

Sin(ful) translates from the Greek word *hamartia* which is an archery term that means "to miss the mark." In Hebrew, the word for sin is *khatta'ah* (root: *chata*) which means "to miss the way/path." The original intent of the word, then, pertains more to *direction*, than specific behavior. Sin, or movement away from the target (i.e., God), has only one destination: Chaos. Pairing Peter's statement of, "I am a sinful man" with this original understanding of the word, then, certainly helps to explain the Peter who is revealed in the Gospel stories: *He who often missed the mark.* For example, in the walking on water story, we saw first-hand how his directionally wayward tendencies plunged him right back into the chaos.

For us, at least two shifts in understanding can take place when we understand and employ the word *sin* with its original meaning,.

1. We are reminded that seeking God is not about choosing sides in the cosmic battle between good and evil, but about choosing to live either in the reign of God (dry land) or in the chaos (the formless void)

2. We are reminded that seeking God is a journey that requires a travel agent (Jesus) and guide (the Holy Spirit) who

are available for consultation – and provide best results when consulted constantly.

RUMINATIONS

Throughout the previous chapters, we've looked at the ways humans attempt to manage and overcome the chaos on their own and then compared these ways with the very different (and often counter-intuitive) path offered by God that, when chosen, sets humans free of the chaos. In the last two chapters, we saw how Jesus embodied this way, the reign of God. The scripture story for this chapter continues with this theme, but does so by way of invitation. Jesus invites Peter, James, and John to follow him and learn how to live free of the chaos.

There's just one problem: The story you picked doesn't have any chaos in it. Why would you end a book about chaos with a story that has no chaos in it?

There is very little *active* chaos in this story. But note the relationship that the soon-to-be disciples have with the sea (*chaos*). For Peter, James, and John, the sea was the source of provision – their work, pay, and food depended on it. But, as reported by Peter in verse 5, the sea was not always reliable.

Sometimes, the fish did not bite and we know from other stories that storms could suddenly appear, bringing hardship and danger.

Which means, when Jesus tells Peter, James, and John to throw their nets out at a time of day when fishing was considered ineffective (which is why the fishermen were washing their nets at that time instead of using them), we are seeing a brief, but interesting, interplay between the people who daily interact with the chaos versus someone who daily walks God's way.

So Jesus wasn't just rewarding Peter, James, and John for loaning him their boat for the morning?

Correct. Jesus wants to demonstrate the effectiveness of God's better way. But initially, Peter is unaware of Jesus' intent, which is probably why Peter sounds less than enthused when he responds to Jesus's suggestion with, "Master, we have worked all night and caught nothing."

I have to say, I'm on Peter's side here. Jesus' suggestion is inconvenient.

Yes, Jesus' suggestion *is* inconvenient. What is surprising, then, is that Peter, despite his grumbling, agrees to do what Jesus says.

Maybe this willingness by Peter to listen and obey is why Jesus called him as a disciple?

Very possible. Additionally, Peter's lack of success from the previous night may have left him feeling dissatisfied with his usual strategies and more receptive to new approaches.

Well, it looks like the new approach worked out for Peter – with boatloads of fish! But once Jesus' way of dealing with the chaos proves so successful, why then does Peter tell Jesus to go away from him?

At a literal level, the amount of fish that Jesus helped Peter catch was significant. It would've been too big of a gift to be received, at least at first. For example, think of someone giving you a brand new house, mortgage-free. No matter how excited you might be by the gift, it would also be difficult to accept.

This is true. If you gave me a (nice) free house, my first response would be, "This is great! Thank you so much! Now take it back."

But on another level, Peter is saying something more profound. He's saying that his way of life (i.e., *sinful*)[48] and Jesus'

---

[48] See the "sin(ful)" entry in the *Concepts* section of this chapter for details about the directional properties of the word, "sin"

way of life are diametrically opposed and that the gulf between their two ways is too large to bridge.

But if that's really what Peter is saying, then how could Jesus' simple response of "from now on you will be catching people" so quickly change Peter's mind?

When Jesus says "from now on you will be catching people," he isn't just making a clever play on words to reassure Peter, James, and John that they have what it takes to be his disciples. Jesus is also explaining how that distance (that Peter sees between him and Jesus) will be bridged.

You've lost me. I don't see an explanation about bridging any distances in Jesus' invitation.

Consider the imagery in Jesus' invitation based upon the type of fishing that Peter, James, and John did. The location of the "catchers" would be above the water (in their boats), which would mean that those who are being caught would be caught from the water – they would either be *in* or *under* the water.

Let's then remember that Peter, James, and John's lives at this point are enmeshed with the sea. Although their close proximity to the shore symbolically hints at their receptivity to leaving the clutches of the chaos, the only life they have known is a life of living in the chaos. In other words, they were not currently positioned (i.e., above the chaos) to catch anyone, but they were correctly positioned to be *caught*.

This brings us to how Jesus' invitation *to* something is also an invitation *away* from something else. You might even say Jesus is *luring* Peter, James, and John away from their chaos-immersed life. By accepting Jesus' invitation to fish for people, then, Peter, James, and John are also simultaneously choosing to leave the chaos. In other words, to follow Jesus is the equivalent of a fish being pulled from the water. This is how Jesus' invitation would (and does) bridge the distance between him and Peter, James, and John.

So they bought it hook, line, and sinker – sorry, I couldn't resist! But in all seriousness, doesn't pulling a fish from the water result in the death of the fish? How could this invitation possibly appeal to Peter, James, and John?

At this point, it is important to note two aspects where Jesus' clever analogy should not be taken to extremes.

First, a person cannot be forcefully removed from the chaos in the same way a fish can be forcefully removed from the sea. A person must make their own choice to leave the chaos.

And second, removing a fish from the water will kill it. But a person choosing to be removed from a chaos-centered life will *not* be killed.

However, leaving a chaos-centered life will *feel* like a death, which is a theme that Jesus mentions at various points in his ministry ("You must lose your life to gain it," for example). Instead of dying, though, a person would transition to living in and experiencing God's kingdom.

This, then, is the invitation Jesus offers Peter, James, and John: To enter and inhabit the environment where they were made to live.

As you talk about this, I'm starting to rethink my assumption that the line, "they left everything" was an exaggeration.

Good! When Peter, James and John "left everything and followed Jesus," they weren't just leaving family, responsibilities, jobs, possessions, relationships, and a freshly-caught pile of fish. They were also leaving behind the techniques, habits, and routines that defined their daily chaos-surviving life. They were walking away from everything that defined them. Again, though they do not die like a fish removed from the sea, the closest analogy to this type of transition *is* physical death.

You *do* know that this choice sounds a lot less appealing when you talk about it being a type of death, right? I'm very sure that my life isn't so bad that I need to experience a type of death to make it better. Why would I – or anyone else – ever make this same choice to follow Jesus like Peter, James, and John did?

This is an incredibly important question! It is so important, in fact, that no one can answer it for you. However, that does not mean you have to arrive at your answer in a vacuum or by yourself. In fact, the purpose of this book has been to help you consider your answer to this question.

Well, if that's the case, would you summarize the book and then explain how it helps me consider my answer?

Gladly!

First, we viewed the original design of creation as presented by Genesis. We compared it to more conventional understandings (at the time) of creation (represented by the *Enuma Elish*) and saw a startling difference in perspective: The Hebrew story of creation depicted God as one who did not wade in and fight the chaos, but instead hovered over it and transformed it, not with violence or explosions, but with words and reason. God's original design was functional, ordered, purposeful, and attractive. It was not, and is not, a slap-dash product of randomly dispersed spoils of war. And it wasn't just good, it was *very* good.

We then read in the Noah story how life lived apart from God leads us to misplace the chaos, thus corrupting our living condition and undoing our environment. But Noah, who sought to walk with God, received instructions that kept him above the chaos – similar to how God's Holy Spirit hovered over it in the beginning.

In the parting of the Red Sea story, we were introduced to the *mitsrayim*, a management system designed by humans to control the chaos. However, we saw how the *mitsrayim* did not control, manage, or order the chaos, but *displaced* the chaos. By displacing a disproportionate share of the chaos onto the most vulnerable members of society, the *mitsrayim* (a.k.a. Egypt/Empire) used weaker and less-fortunate humans as buffers to keep the benefactors of *mitsrayim* mostly free of the chaos.

But the *mitsrayim*, just like any other human attempt to control the chaos, eventually fails. Pharaoh's ending was the same as Noah's neighbors: He was consumed by the chaos while the Israelites - who took the time to be still and listen for God's direction - walked on dry land.

The last three stories we read featured Jesus, an embodiment of God's reign. Just as Noah and Moses followed God's unconventional approach to the chaos, so did Jesus. He walked above it, he calmed it, he fished it, and when it screamed at him, he named it and returned it to where it belonged. The results of Jesus' approach strongly contrast with the results of the people who were immersed in the chaos. Peter literally sank into it, James and John went a whole night without catching any fish, and the Gerasene demoniac, an embodiment of chaos, was unable to control even his own body.

Throughout the scripture stories, then, the message is consistent and clear: We are made to live on dry land and breathe the air (*ruach / spirit / kingdom of God*). But then we invite the chaos into places it does not belong and let it stay. We then think we can manage it and live in it, but instead, we are constantly overwhelmed by it. To make things worse, as we struggle against the chaos without God's direction and help, we create oppressive systems, even when we mean well. In this way, the road to a chaotic hell has been, is, and will continue to be paved with good intentions.

But this was never God's intent for us. We were designed to be *ruach*-breathers, not *chaos*-breathers. But to become *ruach*-breathers, each of us must say, "No" to living in the chaos and say, "Yes" to living in the reign of God.

Alright! I'm convinced! I do not want to live in the chaos or participate in the oppressive systems of *mitsrayim*. I'm ready to leave my chaos-centered life. I want to be a *ruach*–breather, not a *chaos*-breather! How do I sign up!?

By accepting Jesus' invitation to daily follow him and fish for people. But to be fishers of people, to be God's gifts in the chaos of this world, we must first evolve from *chaos*-breathers to *ruach*-breathers. This daily journey of personal change is what it means to be a disciple of Jesus.

As disciples of Jesus, we learn to let go of our techniques, habits, and routines of living in the chaos. In their place, we also learn to live in the reign of God like Jesus did. We learn to admit that we cannot manage or navigate or stop the chaos on our own. We learn to listen in prayer for God's direction even in the midst of the chaos. We learn to then surrender to and trust God's direction instead of trusting our seven (in)effective habits. In essence, we are daily reborn to live a new way, a way where we've learned to move above the chaos instead of being immersed in it.

This is the choice before us, then, when Jesus says, "Follow me." And, it's a big one. As Moses told the Israelites, "I have set before you life and death, blessings and curses. Choose life."[49]

---

[49] Deuteronomy 30:19

I accept! I choose life!

Good to hear! But do not think that everything will be better just because you are choosing to live in the reign of God.

What?! But that's why I just signed-up!

The journey from *mitsrayim* to God's reign will have intense moments of setback and disappointment. We saw this with Noah's drunkenness, the Israelites' desire to return to Egypt ("Were there not enough graves in Egypt that you brought us out here to die?"), Peter's sinking into the sea after successfully walking on water, and the Gerasene townspeople telling Jesus to leave their town.

Furthermore, the more you move with God's direction, the more you will encounter the disdain, resistance, and even murderous intent by the ensconced benefactors of the *mitsrayim*. You will no longer be one of them. Instead, you will be a threat to their approach to surviving the chaos and they *will* turn on you.

This choice, then, is not an easy one. The immediate rewards are few and far between. You will lose a great amount in making and then living this decision. The cost of this decision is what Jesus is referring to in the parables of the king who does his calculations before going to war and the merchant who sells everything he owns to buy that one pearl.[50] In other words, be very sure you know what you are choosing.

I see. So maybe I should more carefully consider my decision. Can I learn more before I choose to actually become a disciple?

Of course you can! An informed decision is the best decision.

Okay, let's say that I *have* been more considerate in my decision, and that I now know that I'm ready to follow Jesus. How do I actually do that?

That, dear reader, is another conversation for another book. But it is one that we want to have with you, which is why we're hard at work on our next book in the *Reign of God* series. Look for updates about our progress on the www.rfour.org site.

Wait – You're just going to leave me hanging like that? With an *advertisement* for another one of your books!?

The primary source that we use for the words and ideas in this book, and any other book we write, is the Bible. We strongly recommend that you read and study the four Gospels (Matthew, Mark, Luke and John) and the book of Acts – preferably with

---

[50] Luke 14:30-33 and Matthew 13:45-46

others, like the group with whom you have been reading this book.

Why those five books?

The Gospels and the Book of Acts narrate the start, middle, and end of the discipleship process. If you want some guidance and help with leading a Bible study, we invite you to use the free Bible study guides we will be posting on rfour.org. It is a bit of a process to edit and prepare those study guides, so they may not all be finished when you visit, but there will certainly be enough there to get you started. There will also be relevant audio messages (i.e., Michael's sermons) available as another resource to help you daily choose to live in the reign of God.

So that's it? We're all done? No more witty and clever banter?

If you have questions or comments or stories to share with us, you can find our contact information on the rfour.org website.

I admit that I have been challenged by our discussions in this book. And, I'm not sure I even agree with all that you've said – mostly because a lot of it so new and different from what I've previously heard and learned. But I have really

appreciated your honesty and insights. Thank you! I look forward to doing this again. Until next time, then?

Until next time, then, dear reader. In the meantime, we pray for God's love, light, blessing, wisdom, healing, and strength for you as you seek first the reign of God.

Michael & Nathanael

Suggested Outline for
CLASS DISCUSSION

1. **Opening Prayer** (1 to 2 minutes)

2. **Opening Question** (10 minutes): *Is there any invitation or offer that would strongly entice you to quickly (within a week of the offer) pack up and leave the life that you are currently living (you can take your immediate family with you, but not your friends and not most of your things)? If yes, what offer would entice you?*

3. **Read the chapter's scripture passage**

4. **Discussion** (30 to 35 minutes):

   a) Share with the group one or two points in the Context, Scripture Reading, Concepts, and Ruminations sections that you appreciated, disagreed with, struggled to accept or didn't understand.

b) *"In other words, following Jesus is the equivalent of a fish being pulled from the water."* Have you ever heard of discipleship and following Jesus described this way? What is it about this description that appeals to you? What is it about this description that does not appeal to you?

c) *"Why would I ever make this same choice to follow Jesus like Peter, James, and John did?"* As you consider choosing to be a follower of Jesus, what's the best thing that you think could happen if you make this choice?

d) *"But do not think that everything will be better just because you are choosing to live in the reign of God."* What promises have you previously heard you would receive if you lived God's way?

e) *"Because an informed decision is the best decision."* Do you think this book has helped you better understand why you would want to (or already do) follow Jesus? If yes, in what ways?

f) *Follow-up to Question E:* What else do you think you would like to know about making the choice to follow

Jesus? And, how might you plan to find that needed information?

5. **What's next**: Brainstorm with the group what you would like to do next, if anything. *Suggestions*: a Bible study, pairing up with a prayer partner, or creating a way to support each other as disciples committed to living in the reign of God.

6. **Closing Prayer** (3 to 7 minutes)

REFERENCE LIST

1. A Far Country—Decapolis. (n.d.). Retrieved from http://followtherabbi.com/guide/detail/a-far-country-decapolis

2. Anesi, C. The Titanic Casualty Figures and What They Mean. Retrieved from March 26, 2013 from http://www.anesi.com/titanic.htm

3. Bar-Ilan, M. Illiteracy in the Land of Israel in the first centuries c.e. Retrieved from https://faculty.biu.ac.il/~barilm/illitera.html

4. Blank, W. (n.d.). Gadarenes. Retrieved from http://www.keyway.ca/ htm2003/20030210.htm

5. Bratcher, D. Genesis Bible Study - Lesson Two: The Cultural Context of Israel. Retrieved July 14, 2014, from The Voice. http://www.cresourcei.org/biblestudy/bbgen2.html

6. Brueggemann, W. Theology of the Old Testament: Testimony, Dispute, Advocacy (Minneapolis: Fortress, 1997), 74-75.

7. Chaos. (n.d.) Biblegateway.com. Retrieved July 7, 2014 from https://www.biblegateway.com/resources/dictionary-of-bible-themes/4045-chaos

8. Chaos. (n.d.). Encyclopedia Mythica. Retrieved from http://www.pantheon.org/articles/c/chaos.html

9. Davies, G.I (1998). "Introduction to the Pentateuch". In John Barton. Oxford Bible Commentary. Oxford University Press. ISBN 9780198755005.

10. Enns, P. (2012). When Was Genesis Written And Why Does it Matter: A Brief Historical Study. http://biologos.org/uploads/ resources/ enns_scholarly_essay3.pdf, 9-10.

11. Enns, P. Yahweh, Creation, and the Cosmic Battle. Retrieved July 17, 2014, from BioLogos. http://biologos.org/blog/yahweh-creation-and-the-cosmic-battle

12. Evans, C. Jewish Scripture and the Literacy of Jesus (p48). Retrieved from http://www.craigaevans.com/evans.pdf

13. Greenwold, D. (2008). Being a First-Century Disciple. Retrieved from https://bible.org/article/being-first-century-disciple

14. Hellenism: Center of the Universe. (n.d.). Retrieved from http://followtherabbi.com/guide/detail/hellenism-center-of-the-universe

15. How should we interpret the Genesis flood account? (n.d.). Retrieved from http://biologos.org/questions/ genesis-flood#detail

16. Isaak, M. Problems with a Global Flood (Second Edition). Retrieved July 1, 2014, from TalkOrigins Archive. http://www.talkorigins.org/faqs/faq-noahs-ark.html#implications

17. Jacobsen, T. [1968]. "The Battle between Marduk and Tiamat". Journal of the American Oriental Society 88 (1): 105.

18. Johnson, M. The Sea as a Symbol of the Powers of Chaos in the Hebrew Scriptures. Retrieved July 10, 2014, from http://graceofamador.org/ Sea%20as%20an%20emblem%20of%20chaos%20in%20the %20OT.pdf

19. Kogler, K. (2009). Disciples in the First Century. Retrieved from http://theequipper.org/downloads/PDFs/Disciples.pdf Pg 51.

20. Rabbi and Talmidim: Education in Galilee. (n.d.). Retrieved from http://followtherabbi.com/guide/detail/rabbi-and-talmidim

21. Ruwach. (n.d.) BibleStudyTools.com. Retrieved from http://www.biblestudytools.com/lexicons/hebrew/kjv/ruwa ch-2.html

22. Seiglie, M. The Bible and Archaeology: The Red Sea or the Reed Sea? Good News Magazine May - June 1997. http://www.ucg.org/science/bible-and-archaeology-red-sea-or-reed-sea/

23. Tsar. (Brown-Driver-Briggs) Biblehub.com. Retrieved July 7, 2014 from http://biblehub.com/bdb/6862.htm

24. Webster, M. (2001). Enuma Elish--The Babylonian Creation Story. http://faculty.gvsu.edu/websterm/Enuma_Elish.html

25. Yahweh's Conflict with the Leviathan and the Sea (n.d.) Retrieved July 7, 2014, from Knowing the Bible.net. https://www.knowingthebible.net/yahweh-the-leviathan-and-sea

26. Young, E. The Symoblism of the Word "Mitzrayim" (Egypt). Etz Hayim. Retrieved July 7, 2014 from http://www.etz-hayim.com/resources/articles/mitzrayim.php

About the Authors

Michael T. Bush is the Senior Pastor of the United Church of Christ at Valley Forge in suburban Philadelphia. He has served as an ordained minister in the United Church of Christ for over 20 years, including churches in the Seattle area, Michigan, and Connecticut. He holds a B.S. in Biology (pre-med) from the University of Michigan, a M. Div. from Christian Theological Seminary in Indianapolis, and has participated in continuing education terms at Lancaster Theological Seminary & Yale Divinity School. He is committed to a ministry of renewal among the Body of Christ through Biblical literacy, theological reflection, and spiritual practices.

Nathanael Vissia has a B.A. in English and has taught in churches, public schools, camps, and college. To address what he perceived as a lack of quality Sunday school lessons, he launched www.rfour.org in 2011 as a support website for Christian Educators. It offers over 200 of his lessons, 100+ children's sermons, and various other resources – including additional resources available for *Chaos & the Kingdom* and soon-to-be-added Bible study notes for adults – all for free. As of 2015, the site is ranked #1 in numerous Google and Bing searches, most notably for "Middle School Sunday lessons" & "Confirmation lessons."

Made in the USA
San Bernardino, CA
22 March 2020

66196658R00093